INSTRUCTIONAL ALIGNMENT

Optimizing Objectives, Methods, and Assessment for Developing Unit Plans

Suzanne Houff

Rowman & Littlefield Education

A division of
ROWMAN & LITTLEFIELD PUBLISHERS, INC.
Lanham • New York • Toronto • Plymouth, UK

Published by Rowman & Littlefield Education
A division of Rowman & Littlefield Publishers, Inc.
A wholly owned subsidiary of The Rowman & Littlefield Publishing Group, Inc.
4501 Forbes Boulevard, Suite 200, Lanham, Maryland 20706
www.rowman.com

10 Thornbury Road, Plymouth PL6 7PP, United Kingdom

Copyright © 2012 by Suzanne Houff

All rights reserved. No part of this book may be reproduced in any form or by any electronic or mechanical means, including information storage and retrieval systems, without written permission from the publisher, except by a reviewer who may quote passages in a review.

British Library Cataloguing in Publication Information Available

Library of Congress Cataloging-in-Publication Data

Houff, Suzanne G., 1953–
  Instructional alignment : optimizing objectives, methods, and assessment for developing unit plans / Suzanne Houff.
    p. cm.
  Summary: "In response to a quagmire of jargon based and convoluted curriculum textbooks, 'Instructional Alignment' offers a concise and basic approach to instructional design. By exploring the areas of planning, assessment, and methodology, this text outlines the essential components of effective teaching and illustrates how they align in order to maximize student learning"— Provided by publisher.
  ISBN 978-1-60709-453-1 (pbk.) — ISBN 978-1-60709-454-8 (electronic)
 1. Instructional systems—Design. 2. Curriculum planning. I. Title.
 LB1028.38.H68 2012
 371.3—dc23   2012025048

"There is a principle which is a bar against all information, which is proof against all arguments, and which cannot fail to keep a man in everlasting ignorance—that principle is contempt prior to investigation."

—Herbert Spencer

CONTENTS

PREFACE	vii
INTRODUCTION	1
1 **PLANNING** Designing a Plan for Effective Instruction	3
2 **ASSESSMENT** Using Assessment to Drive Instruction	17
3 **INSTRUCTION** Instructional Strategies for Maximum Learning	41
4 **ALIGNMENT** A Project-Based Learning Unit	59
APPENDIX A: LESSON PLAN TEMPLATE	69
APPENDIX B: PROJECT-BASED LEARNING UNIT TEMPLATE	71
GLOSSARY	73
REFERENCES	85
ABOUT THE AUTHOR	87

PREFACE

I began writing this book in response to my own questions regarding curriculum and instruction. As I tried to select a textbook for my curriculum and instruction class, I became overwhelmed with terminology, strategies, and designs. I knew that I would never be able to cover all the material in one semester. Furthermore, I could not explain all the information to my students if I did not conceptualize it myself.

Therefore, I began my quest to make sense of and simplify all the pages of information that crowded the textbooks.

I started with what I already knew. I began with Ralph Tyler's *Basic Principles of Curriculum and Instruction* (1949), in which he outlines a very clear and simple design for teaching and learning. In a nutshell, he proposes that effective instruction begins by formulating an objective. This is followed by an organization of instruction that is supported through quality assessment. He suggests the process is ongoing with revisions and redesigns to meet the needs of the learner.

As I struggled through the textbooks, I wondered when it had all become so confusing and overwhelming. It appeared to me that the ideas are basically the same but new names are attached. Good teachers have been practicing these strategies for years.

In summary, this is what I gleaned from my readings: Education can take many forms. There is environmental, character, values, experiential, hands-on, global, holistic, multicultural, and immersion education.

Education can also be cooperative, which is different from cooperative learning. Competencies form the basis of the standards. Standards can be core, content, or state. Some standards are new. Some provide an opportunity to learn. We even have world-class standards. The goals, however, are national.

Objectives are derived from the standards. There are indicators for the outcomes and outcomes to look for measures of performance. The competencies, standards, and objectives are the basis for the essential questions.

Instruction can be designed backward or forward, or even process-based. It can be individualized or differentiated by content, process, or product. Either way, we must ensure that we implement a culturally relevant pedagogy that addresses the twenty-first-century skills. Instruction is not the only aspect of education that is differentiated. We also have differentiated school, staffing, supervision, and teaching.

The curriculum should be aligned but it can also be interdisciplinary, integrated, free choice, multidisciplinary, problem-based, and/or project-based. Sometimes the curriculum is hidden. Other times the curriculum may spiral.

PREFACE

Consideration must be given to how multiple intelligences play into the instructional process. They, however, should not be confused with learning domains or styles. Instruction may be computer assisted. Whatever instructional type is implemented, it should be developmentally appropriate.

Assessment begins with front-end or pre. It includes remedial, needs-based, and outcome-based measurement. Assessment can be alternative and/or authentic. It measures benchmarks, standards, or outcomes. There are performance assessment, performance tasks, and performance criteria. Exhibition of mastery and matrix sampling can be added to the list.

We have achievement, aptitude, standardized, and competence tests; these, however, are different from a placement exam. There are also criterion-based, which are different from criterion-referenced, which are different from norm-referenced.

Learning can be experiential, action, active, interactive, discovery, mastery, or adventure. It may take the form of cooperative, service, affective, cognitive, work-based, blended, or self-directed. Life-long, kinesthetic, and inquiry are additional ways of learning. There is also a community-based type of learning, which is very different from distance learning or computer-based learning. There is now brain-based learning. Isn't that what learning has always been?

If the student needs additional help, there is Response to Intervention.

Now, granted, these are important concepts that help shape quality instruction but they still can be very frustrating to keep up with. Therefore, I have provided a simple clarification of these terms in the glossary found in the back of the text.

As I grapple with the decision regarding what to present to my graduate students, I find that I need to back up and keep it simple. I ask myself the question that all good teachers ask themselves: "What do my students need to know and be able to do?"

The purpose of this book, then, is to help develop a clear understanding of instructional design. I offer a very simplistic view of a very complex and multifaceted process. This text explores the basics. It explores the alignment of objectives, assessment, and instruction.

This simplistic design is cyclical in nature and straightforward in process. It addresses these questions: Where do I want to go? How will I know if I get there? And what is the best route to take?

INTRODUCTION

When I take my car in to get it aligned, my mechanic, Mickey, charges me a great deal of money just to adjust the angles of my front wheels. He does this to reduce the wear and tear of my tires and to ensure a straight travel path. He looks at the specifications of my car and matches his adjustments to meet those needs. When everything is ready, I can set out assured that I will eventually reach my destination. That is, of course, if I know where I am going and how to get there.

Instructional alignment is much the same way. Alignment means that your curriculum and lessons are developed so that you can successfully reach your objective. By looking at the curriculum specifications or standards, you adjust your lessons so they don't narrow or widen the focus in such a manner that instruction is not effective.

The front, or toe, of my car needs to balance with the rear, or camber. As in a car alignment, objectives and assessment need to link with the teaching method in order to have a balanced instruction.

An aligned curriculum suggests that each component of the lesson correlates with the objective and goal. All parts are supported by well-written objectives, quality assessments, and engaging strategies.

This text provides you with a simplistic overview of developing objectives, assessment, and instruction so they align. It addresses the questions you face each time you develop an instructional plan: Where am I going? How will I know if I get there? And what is the best route to take?

Writing quality objectives is the first step in alignment. They provide the foundation and direction for the lesson. This book first looks at establishing objectives for instruction. The chapter on planning and objectives covers the steps involved in taking broad core or state standards and designing them into a meaningful and manageable goals. Taxonomies are discussed to help you form these objectives so that higher-level learning can take place.

This chapter also identifies the type of knowledge covered in an objective. Whether the learning will be procedural, declarative, or disposition plays a big role in developing the plan of instruction. For example, learning to appreciate the need for protecting the environment is a different type of learning than acquiring the knowledge and skill needed to differentiate recycling materials. Therefore, they must be taught differently.

Next, the text investigates the role of assessment. This chapter explores using assessment to drive instruction. Both formative and summative assessment strategies are addressed. You will discover when and how to use both of these assessments to guide instruction.

Pre-assessment guides the instructional process by allowing you to determine what your students know and what they have already mastered. Formative assessment guides instruction with an ongoing determination of the level of learning for each student. Summative evaluation completes the process by allowing you to establish the

INTRODUCTION

degree of mastery for each student. Both formative and summative assessments provide information regarding the next step in the instructional process. They tell you if the student has mastered the information or if it needs to be taught differently.

The assessment chapter guides you through the development of both teacher-made tests and performance assessment. Best practices are identified and described to provide you with an opportunity to both explore and learn implementation strategies.

The instruction chapter investigates different ways to meet your objectives through a variety of direct and indirect teaching strategies. This chapter explores methods to keep students engaged and motivated during instruction.

The best instructional strategy to use is based on the established learning objective. Depending on the type of learning to take place and the objective to be reached, instructional methods will vary. The instruction chapter explores these approaches under three headings: inductive, social, and independent.

Inductive strategies include approaches that are more constructivist in nature. This type of learning indicates that students are actively involved in developing meaning. Concepts discussed for inductive learning include concept attainment and inquiry-based concepts.

The social instructional method fosters learning through student collaboration. This group effort may come in the form of cooperative discussions, panels and debates, and role playing.

The chapter concludes with a focus on independent instructional approaches. These strategies include learning centers and contracts. The chapter investigates ways to employ these in the classroom and offers suggestions for their development.

Case studies help summarize each chapter. The case studies focus on the chapter topic and offer an opportunity to apply the chapter content. The situations described could easily apply to any classroom. The scenario is followed by questions that are developed to provide you with possible solutions to the situation outlined. They present practical application to the ideas covered in each chapter.

The final chapter brings all the components together for unit planning. Each area of alignment—planning, assessment, and instruction—is described and illustrated in the development of a unit plan. Using a project-based learning design, you will explore integrating twenty-first-century skills in a unit of study. The theme of recycling is used to illustrate the process and clarify the development. Figures in this chapter clearly delineate the steps by using examples and templates.

This book attempts to deliver a simple and clear process for effective instructional alignment. It provides a simplistic and clear explanation for each of the curriculum components of planning, assessment, and instruction. The goal is to help you map out your instructional journey.

PLANNING

Designing a Plan for Effective Instruction

OPTIMIZING PLANNING

Standards—Goals—Objectives

You probably would not go on a trip without some type of planning. Besides planning for expenses, clothing, and lodging, you need to decide where you are going and how you are going to get there. If you don't know where you are going, you probably won't arrive at the right place. Through instructional planning, you answer the question, "Where am I going?"

Planning increases the effectiveness of the lesson and the manageability of your classroom.

The first step in lesson design is deciding what your students need to know and be able to do. What goals do you want and need to meet? What learning objectives will help meet the goal? Let's take a look at some of these learning destinations.

Standards are goals or expectations. They target student learning in specific subjects. When we discuss standard-based curriculum, we refer to a curriculum that is designed to meet the core, state, or organizational required knowledge, skills, and dispositions. The standards are specifically outlined based on agreed-upon and established requirements. They provide a purpose for the learning journey and establish a destination.

Goals are based on the standards and written as broad statements. They identify general learning outcomes for students. They express what learning will take place. These broad goals provide a framework for the more focused and specific objectives.

Objectives are the steps that students need to take in order to reach the goals. They are written as narrow and specific statements.

For example, you might have a standard that states, "The student will (TSW) use meaning clues and language structure when reading." More specifically, based on this standard, your goals for the student might include the following:

TSW
use information in the story to read words
use knowledge of sentence structure
use knowledge of story structure and sequence

Both the standard and goal are very broad and do not list specific skills or actions. To go back to the journey analogy, it would be like saying I want to go to Fredericksburg, Virginia. You know where you want to go but you aren't sure how to get there.

You need specific directions or objectives for your journey. Your objective for the previous standard and goal might include the following:

TSW
use prior knowledge to interpret pictures and diagrams in order to predict text
use meaning clues to support decoding
use surrounding words in a sentence to determine the meaning of a word
use the context of the sentence to distinguish which of the multiple meanings of a word makes sense
use knowledge of word order, including subject, verb, and adjectives, to check for meaning
use story structure, titles, pictures, and diagrams to check for meaning, and reread to clarify meaning

The objectives provide a specific route to take in order to meet the goal or standard.

Practice

Read the following science standard:

The student will investigate and understand characteristics and interactions of moving objects. Key concepts of this science standard might include the following:

- Motion is described as an object's direction and speed
- Forces cause changes in motion
- Friction is a force that opposes motion
- Moving objects have kinetic energy

Based on this standard and key concept, what might your classroom goal be? It would need to include topics related to the key concepts involving motion, forces, friction, and kinetic energy.

What specific objectives would students meet in order to achieve the goal? Objectives narrow the concept focus even more. They could be stated as follows:

TSW
define *motion* as an object's direction and speed
demonstrate a change in motion using force
describe *friction* as a force that opposes motion
explain kinetic energy

The objectives clearly establish what the student will know and be able to do, think, or feel.

But we are getting ahead of ourselves. First, we need to decide what kind of trip we are taking. Are we going on a learning trip for the students to gain knowledge, learn a procedure, or develop an attitude? We base our specific steps or objectives on the purpose or goal of this learning trip. Is the purpose to acquire knowledge (declarative), skill (procedural), or disposition (attitude)?

Knowledge—Skill—Disposition

Declarative knowledge is information based. For example, "TSW know five reasons for the 'going green' initiative." This is knowledge or information they have acquired.

Procedural knowledge is skill or process based. "TSW demonstrate practices in 'going green.'" The students demonstrate a skill they have gained. They demonstrate procedures.

Disposition is the acquisition of an attitude. "TSW appreciate the need to become environmentally responsible." This objective is based on a feeling or disposition that the student will acquire.

Exercise 1.1

Look at the following objectives. Which objectives are knowledge based? Skill based? Disposition based?

TSW
name the keys on the piano
solve long-division problems
appreciate the classroom diversity
identify the main character in a fictional story
develop a PowerPoint presentation
write a complete sentence
describe photosynthesis
value the characteristics of a democratic government

Did you find any objectives that could possibly be more than one type of learning? Think about long division. Wouldn't students need to have knowledge of multiplication tables? They would also need to understand the procedure to follow for long division.

Identifying the type of knowledge the students gain helps you determine how to state your objective, plan assessment, and design instruction.

Taxonomies

After you have identified the type of learning that needs to take place, you can start to write the objectives. Taxonomies offer a means of classifying the outcome. They help you identify the level or degree of difficulty of your objective. How you state the objective indicates its level of complexity.

CHAPTER 1

We are going to look at three different taxonomies. The first taxonomy deals with levels of thinking.

In 1956, Benjamin Bloom provided educators with a taxonomy of intellectual behavior and higher-order thinking skills. This taxonomy outlined levels of cognition with knowing identified as the lowest level of thinking. This hierarchy of skills continued with comprehending, applying, analyzing, synthesizing, and evaluating (the highest level of thinking). Based on verbs associated with each level, teachers could identify the level of thinking for each objective.

During the 1990s, the taxonomy underwent a revision and update to better meet the needs of the twenty-first-century learner. This revised taxonomy, as seen in table 1.1, offers a continuum of thinking skills that provide a foundation for objective development.

Table 1.1. Bloom's Revised Taxonomy of Intellectual Behavior: Cognitive Domain

Level	Explanation	Verb
creating	constructing new elements	generate, invent, design
evaluating	making judgments	argue, critique, hypothesize
analyzing	examining the whole to find relationships	differentiate, interrogate, compare
applying	using information in a different situation	interpret, execute, implement
understanding	interpreting ideas or thoughts	explain, identify, classify
remembering	recalling information	list, describe, memorize

Remembering is the least difficult task, while creating is the most complicated. It is much easier to remember that ice is frozen water than it is to evaluate the process of freezing water. Creating an alternative method to freezing rather than putting water in the freezer would require a more intense level of processing information.

The taxonomy dealing with procedures and processes is usually referred to as the psychomotor domain. This area addresses skills that at times use both the mind and body. Table 1.2 outlines the levels in this domain as identified by Anita Harrow's (1972) psychomotor taxonomy. An explanation and education example is provided with each level. As indicated in this taxonomy, skilled movement in a physical activity is much more advanced than a movement that is reflex. Deliberately catching and returning a thrown ball is a more complex and deliberate act than a reflexive throwing up of arms in avoidance of an oncoming ball.

The most complex skill in this taxonomy deals with body language and the ability to deliberately and in a straightforward manner deliver a message through body movements and facial expressions.

Table 1.3 focuses on the taxonomy of disposition or the affective domain. Outcomes based on this taxonomy apply to attitudes, beliefs, and value systems. Adapted from D. R. Krathwohl's (1964) taxonomy of educational objectives, this chart provides an overview of the levels through an explanation and verbs that indicate performance.

On receiving, or the lowest level, the outcome deals with awareness. The individual becomes cognizant of an issue.

When students respond, they show some new behaviors as a result of the new awareness. For example, students might read a book about "going green." They may even ask or respond to questions about the topic. In addition, they may perform an Internet search or look for another book about "going green."

Table 1.2. Taxonomy of Process and Procedure: Psychomotor Domain

Level	Explanation	Verb
effective communication through body language	providing understandable messages through the use of facial expressions, posture, or hand movements	role play, pantomime
practiced and mastered physical performance	learned complex physical activity as in throwing a baseball or gymnastics	decoding words, perform
physical endurance	maintained strenuous endurance found in weight lifting or marathon running	(not usually seen in educational setting)
coordinated perceptual activities	perceptual-based adjustments directed to accomplish a physical task such as climbing stairs or jumping a fence	write, type
basic movement	essential body movements that allow complex movements to develop such as running or walking	stand, walk
natural physical responses	reaction to physical needs such as stretching or bending	rest, stretch

Table 1.3. Taxonomy of Disposition: Affective Domain

Level	Explanation	Verbs
characterize	adopt values and act accordingly	resolve, display, exhibit
organize	relate new values to self	balance, decide, theorize
value	place an importance on idea	support, help, argue
respond	react to new ideas	applaud, discuss, practice
receive	willing to take in new ideas	listen, notice, attend

Valuing shows some definite involvement or commitment. The individual demonstrates a willingness of dedication.

At the organization level, students integrate a new value into their current value system. They give it some priority in their current beliefs or behaviors.

When students reach the characterization level, they develop behaviors that consistently demonstrate the new behavior. The students are loyal to the new idea.

Using the "going green" theme, let's see how this would look in each taxonomy and in each level. Tables 1.4, 1.5, and 1.6 provide examples outlining each level in the taxonomy and a corresponding objective.

Table 1.4. Going Green Knowledge Taxonomy

Level	Objective (The student will . . .)
creating	construct a school plan for "going green."
evaluating	defend the practice of "going green."
applying	compare "going green" to current school practices.
analyzing	find methods of "going green."
understanding	describe ways to "go green."
remembering	define the phrase "going green."

Table 1.5. Going Green Procedure Taxonomy

Level	Objective (The student will . . .)
effective communication through body language	pantomime the pros and cons of recycling.
practiced and mastered physical performance	perform a recycling dance.
physical endurance	(not usually seen in educational setting)
coordinated perceptual activities	develop a recycling bin.
basic movement	carry materials to be recycled.
natural physical responses	avoid sharp objects.

Table 1.6. Going Green Disposition Taxonomy

Level	Objective (The student will . . .)
characterize	consistently demonstrate "going green" behaviors and become the leader of a "going green" club in the school.
organize	arrange a "going green" day at school.
value	become involved in encouraging other students to recycle.
respond	begin to practice behaviors associated with "going green" as a result of the demonstration.
receive	pay attention to a demonstration on "going green."

Writing the Objective

Once you have decided what type of learning needs to take place, you now can determine the specific focus or objective. You write the objective based on the purpose of the learning. What do you want students to know and be able to think, feel, or do?

To write the objective, you are going to focus on three components: the content, type of learning, and level of learning. Only by identifying these three areas can you later develop an assessment that adequately determines if the objective is met. Only by aligning the objective and assessment can you later decide the best instructional method. Each stage is built on the previous development.

Let's say your objective is this: "TSW correctly identify and sort the contents of the classroom garbage container according to recycling categories."

The content deals with the subject matter that you want to teach. For the previous objective, the content is recycling.

The type of learning refers to declarative (knowledge), procedural (skill), or disposition (attitude). For the objective above, the type of learning is declarative since the student must have the knowledge of recycling categories and what type of garbage goes in each.

The level of learning for this objective is based on the verb behaviors of *identify* and *sort*. In this case, according to the taxonomies, the level of learning would be *comprehension*.

Identifying the level of learning is important since it allows you to notice if most of your goals focus on lower levels of learning. By knowing the level of learning, you will be able to strive for higher levels and not get stuck in the knowledge and comprehension levels of learning.

The objective matrix found in table 1.7 helps dissect and clarify the objective and identify the content and level of learning.

Table 1.7. Objective Matrix

TSW correctly identify and sort the contents of the classroom garbage container according to recycling categories.

Content	Knowledge	Verb	Level
recycling for "going green"	declarative	identify and sort	cognitive-understanding psychomotor–basic fundamental

Exercise 1.2

Read the following objectives. Using table 1.8, identify the content knowledge, verb, and level for each.

TSW
name the keys on the piano
solve long-division problems
appreciate the classroom diversity
identify the main character in a fictional story
develop a PowerPoint presentation
write a complete sentence
describe photosynthesis
value the characteristics of a democratic government

The objective is the focal point of the learning process. It drives all other aspects of the lesson plan.

Table 1.8.

Content	Type of Knowledge	Verb	Level of Learning

CHAPTER 1

The Lesson Plan

The lesson plan is a map of the objective that you have established. It provides clear directions in order to reach the desired destination. A template for a lesson plan can be found in appendix A. This template allows you to map out the instructional process. By writing out each section of the plan, you are able to clearly see the process and clearly align each component. By placing the standard(s) on the left-hand side and the objective(s) directly across from the standard(s), you can better determine if they correlate.

Summative assessment immediately follows the objectives to emphasize the importance of aligning the assessment with the objective.

The next section on the lesson plan form is designed specifically to indicate the twenty-first-century skills as identified by Partnership for 21st Century Skills (2004). These skills will be further explored in the final chapter.

Pre-assessment allows you to identify what your students already know. This important step will guide your differentiation of instruction. It also provides you a starting point that allows you to better measure individual growth for each student.

The instructional sequence of strategies and formative assessment strategies are placed side by side so that you can easily check for understanding after the introduction and practice of a concept.

Several factors influence how you organize steps in your plan. The content, student level, time available, school resources, and mandated curriculum all affect how and what you plan. Your personal teaching style and beliefs about how students learn also play a role in planning.

The major part of the alignment is making sure assessment directly measures the stated objective. We will look at assessment in the next chapter.

Planning Points to Remember

- Standards are usually established by an organization.
- Goals are based on the standards and describe in a general way what the student needs to know or be able to think, feel, or do.
- Objectives narrow the focus of the goal and are based on the type of learning that will take place.
- Learning can be in the form of acquired knowledge (declarative), a skill (procedural), or a disposition (attitude).
- Taxonomies provide a means to measure the difficulty of a task or learning.
- Assessment can easily be developed when objectives are written in specific behavioral terms.
- Lesson plans provide a map or direction for the instructional process.
- Lesson plans explain what type of pre-assessment is used. Objectives and standards are identified and linked to a summative assessment. The instructional process includes a plan for formative assessment as well as clearly identified strategies that engage learners.

ANSWERS: EXERCISE 1.1

Verb	Type
name	knowledge
solve	knowledge procedure
appreciate	knowledge disposition
identify	knowledge procedure
develop	knowledge procedure
write	knowledge procedure
describe	knowledge
value	knowledge disposition

ANSWERS: EXERCISE 1.2

Content	Type of Knowledge	Verb	Level of Learning
piano keys	declarative	name	remembering
division	procedural and declarative	solve	applying
diversity	disposition	appreciate	valuing
fictional characters	declarative	identify	understanding
PowerPoint presentation	procedural	develop	skilled movement
complex sentence	declarative	write	understanding
photosynthesis	declarative	describe	analyzing
democratic government	disposition	value	valuing

Disclaimer: The answer to all educational questions is "It depends." I have provided a base answer to the practice activities. However, these are not set in stone and it depends on the rigor of the activity. Creating a PowerPoint presentation could easily be a skilled movement based on the necessary procedures. However, depending on the content of the presentation, it could also be in the cognitive domain in the level of "create."

CHAPTER 1

CASE STUDIES

Garry's Battlefield

Mrs. Dodrill is an experienced teacher of ten years at Garry Elementary School. She has taught fourth grade for the past two years and enjoys helping her students develop their academic skills. Prior to teaching fourth grade, Mrs. Dodrill taught sixth-grade history.

This year Mrs. Dodrill has adapted a sixth-grade project to meet the standards of the fourth-grade history. The objective of the project is to help the students gain a better understanding of the state's role in the Civil War through a more hands-on experience. The project has each student completing research to design a shoebox that will depict important events from the Civil War.

The students will present their shoebox project to the class and report on what they have learned. Each child will get to select a topic and conduct book research in class. Mrs. Dodrill suggests that since Civil War battlefields surround Garry Elementary School, the students should visit the battlefields to gain additional information for their project. She also tells the students that visiting a battlefield is not required. Students will have three weeks to work on the project.

The project will be graded using a rubric that the students help design. Mrs. Dodrill and her class decide the rubric should consist of the following categories: creativity, completeness, neatness, and oral presentation.

As the three weeks pass, Mrs. Dodrill reminds the students to judge their progress on the project.

Mrs. Dodrill makes sure that she arranges for students to go to the library to find books. She also sets aside classroom time for students to work.

At the beginning of the third week of the project, Mrs. Dodrill decides to ask Danny to show her his progress on the project. He pulls out an empty shoebox that has only been covered in brown paper. Then he pulls out the research that he has conducted. His research consists only of three sentences. Discouraged by Danny's progress, Mrs. Dodrill suggests that Danny work with another student to complete his research.

Frustrated, Mrs. Dodrill checks on Melissa's progress. Melissa has completed two pages of research, but she is having trouble deciding on what is important to include in her shoebox. Mrs. Dodrill looks over Melissa's research with her and realizes Melissa has included information that is not very important. When questioned, Melissa explains that she had trouble deciding what was important and what was not important.

Finally, the deadline arrives and the children begin to present their projects. Melissa goes first. Her shoebox is plain and includes mainly small details about the battle. Her shoebox decorations are minimal, mostly hand-drawn pictures that correspond to the research she conducted in class. Her report, however, is very impressive. She explains all of the details on her box and shows an exceptional understanding of the state's role in the Civil War.

When it is Danny's turn, he presents a shoebox decorated with pictures of the battlegrounds, small typed excerpts of facts, figurines of important state figures, and a small simulated battleground. His report is very impressive also. The report is typed and uses vocabulary that is well beyond what Danny uses in class. Mrs. Dodrill suspects that Danny did not complete this project himself and that his father did it for him. She decides to ask Danny a few questions about his report. As she suspects, Danny can't answer the questions without referring back to the captions underneath the pictures.

Mrs. Dodrill now has to assign grades for the projects. She decides to score Melissa with full credit in all criteria. When she assigns Danny's grade, she decides that she must give him full credit on all criteria except oral presentation.

Questions to Consider

1. *What problems do you see in Mrs. Dodrill's lesson?*

She has not assigned an assessment that meets the objective. This case does not offer an explanation as to how the shoebox demonstrates an understanding of the state's role in the Civil War.

There is a definite lack of planning for the project. The students lack guidance in their research portion. They seem to not know what to research and what information they must have. Did she assign specific battles that are connected to the state's role? Do the students have to identify the state's role in the shoebox?

Mrs. Dodrill should check students' progress before the third and final week of the project. Although she has planned places and times for the research, she has not provided guidance and structure for the project or the research.

2. *Do you agree with the grading areas for the rubric? Why or why not?*

Answers will vary but they should mention establishing criteria for each of the categories. The number of points for each area should be given.

3. *How could Mrs. Dodrill have better planned for the project?*

She needed to start with a specific objective. From there, she needed to determine how the assignment will demonstrate mastery of the objective. Once she aligned the objective and the assignment, she could develop specific instructional sessions including the names of battles.

She also needed to help design the rubric in order to provide specific criteria for grading.

CHAPTER 1

A Salty Situation

Ms. Jones has been a third-grade teacher for three years, and before that a second-grade teacher for two years. She is liked by her fellow teachers and is known for her motivation skills. She has an ability to engage students who usually lack drive and initiative.

Her students genuinely like and trust her. She returns the feelings.

Her classroom is well managed with schedules as well as jobs for her students.

Ms. Jones takes great pride in her efforts to carefully choose instructional strategies to use in the classroom. She wants to meet the needs of all of her students.

Her third graders are currently learning about ancient Greek civilization and have been for a few weeks now. They had numerous lectures and activities, but they were looking forward to making the salt map. Ms. Jones discussed it for over a week, building up the students' excitement. They discussed maps and terrain and the importance of showing it properly on the salt map. This would be a fun assignment but it would take teamwork to complete and the students would demonstrate their knowledge from the end result of the map. The salt map would be assessed according to whether they listened to directions, whether they demonstrated knowledge of the terrain of ancient Greece and the surrounding areas, and also whether they cooperated with their teams.

The date of the salt map activity was on the calendar and groups had been selected ahead of time.

Two students were not in class the day of the salt map activity; therefore, two groups only had three people versus four. However, all groups completed the salt maps on time during class, and all students were assessed by the teacher at the end of the day. Ms. Jones recorded the grades, comprised mostly of As and a few Bs for students who did not follow directions for washing their hands and cleaning their desks.

The two absent students approached Ms. Jones the following day and Ms. Jones gave them a recap of the salt map activity and told them the make-up work consisted of a worksheet assignment they could take home that evening and complete. Ms. Jones felt this was a fair assignment for the absent students, as she needed a recorded grade for ancient Greece for all her students.

The following day the two students turned in the homework and Ms. Jones graded the assignments after school, noticing that they missed quite a few answers. The students' grades were recorded in the gradebook as Cs and the students were not happy. One student, Mary, chose to speak to Ms. Jones about the grade, stating that it was a difficult and lengthy assignment and the grade was unfair considering how hard it was to complete compared to how easy and fun the salt map project was.

Ms. Jones explained to Mary that the questions on the worksheets were from lectures, class activities, and the textbook. She further explained the information and answers should have been very easy for her since they had been doing ancient Greece for weeks now, and the grade would stand as it was.

The following day Mary came in with a note from her mother stating that she was upset about the grade Mary received and that the graded assignment was unfair since the other students were graded on a map, something completely different from her assignment. Ms. Jones decided to review the worksheet after class to study the questions and answers once more before responding to Mary's mother. She also looked at Joe's homework, which likewise received a C. She compared his answers to Mary's. She found three questions they both missed with the same wrong answers and three questions they both missed with different answers.

Questions to Consider

1. *What problems do you see in the planning of this activity?*

The answers will vary. It seems that Ms. Jones has only planned for one type of assessment—the salt map. It would be more appropriate for students to have multiple types of assessment for the unit. We would need to know what the objectives for the unit were. We would also need to know what activities she has used to meet those objectives. With a unit lasting this long, there must be some type of formative assessment to indicate their learning.

2. *Are two different assignments fair for Ms. Jones to use when grading students that miss class?*

Two different types of assessments are fair in a classroom when students are absent and are unable to make up the exact work as the other students. When giving different assignments, it is important to have the same criteria graded. Ms. Jones's two assignments have different criteria: one is a worksheet full of facts from lectures, activities, and book information, while the other is a salt map showing the terrain of ancient Greece, which also grades the students' teamwork and ability to follow directions. These two assignments do not assess the same information, which makes it difficult to give a comparable grade to the entire class. It also makes it difficult to explain to parents when the criteria the teacher graded on is very different.

3. *Is there a better assignment the teacher could give to the two absent students? Why?*

The fact that two students did a different assignment because they were absent demonstrates that they are taking responsibility for their actions and realizing the consequence when not in class for any reason. However, the assignment seemed to assess different criteria, so giving a comparable grade is difficult. The students who missed class and completed the worksheet for homework did C work, while the teacher gave mostly As to the other students who were in class doing the salt map. This inconsistency in grading does not seem fair and the teacher should address the difference in grades and rethink the assignment, not because it is a different assignment but because they were assessed and graded on different criteria. Possibly the two absent students could work together to complete the salt map.

ASSESSMENT
Using Assessment to Drive Instruction

Assessment is the gathering, evaluating, and using of information before, during, and after instruction. The purpose of assessment is to guide instruction and determine student understanding.

We are going to look at assessment in terms of formative and summative purposes. The strategies discussed are not limited to one type of assessment but can be used as both types of assessments.

FORMATIVE ASSESSMENT

Formative assessment is used during instruction to guide or form your teaching. Used prior to teaching, formative assessment can diagnose students' strengths and weaknesses. This pre-assessment can help you identify skills, knowledge, and dispositions the student already has. It can also establish the needs of the learner. It indicates a starting point for your instruction. You know where to begin instruction through the pre-assessment.

This pre-assessment can be as simple as question-answer recitation or as complex as a multidimensional project. Either way, you need to have a plan for the type of information you need and how you will use that information.

Assessment can also be used to monitor student progress. During instruction, formative assessments help you determine if the student is acquiring the information or mastering the skill. This type of assessment is ongoing and periodic during learning to determine student understanding and progress.

Whatever method is used, continual feedback on progress is essential in developing the student's understanding. This feedback helps guide the instruction and lets students know what they have mastered and what and how they need to improve.

Think back to your own experience with graded assignments. What type of feedback did you receive? What type did you want? What would have been the most helpful to you? What would effective feedback include?

Effective feedback should be stated clearly and in specific terms. It should be grade-level appropriate; in other words, terminology should be easily understood by the student. It should address the specific assignment in a brief and corrective manner. Feedback should be ongoing and criterion-based. For example, *good work* does not provide quality criteria-based feedback to the students concerning their work. No specific characteristics are identified that explain *good*.

CHAPTER 2

Read the following feedback statement given to a student regarding their writing:

"This is a well-written paragraph. You used descriptive words to clearly describe the main character. Each sentence focuses on the main topic of the paragraph."

This feedback identifies what the student did well and what should be repeated in the future. It identifies the criteria. After reading this feedback, the student knows that they stayed with the main topic and used descriptive words. They can identify what they did well.

You might try using a feedback box like the one in table 2.1. It offers a very concise way to summarize the main points of the assignment.

Table 2.1. Feedback Box

FEEDBACK BOX	Points earned:
Strengths of work:	
Opportunities for improvement:	

You can also make a feedback sandwich. Start and end with a positive note about the work. Place the corrective feedback between the two.

Exercise 2.1

Take a look at the following examples. How could the comments be rephrased to offer specific and useful comments?

- Your handwriting is much worse than the rest of the class.
- Your topic sentence is good.
- The work you showed in the math problem indicated that you understood the concept; unfortunately, you made a careless mistake.
- Keep up the good work.
- You used some good adjectives in your description of the science experiment but the findings were wrong.

ASSESSMENT

There are numerous ways to check for understanding using formative assessment. For clarification, the strategies can be further delineated into the areas of talking and gesturing, writing, and making.

Talking and Gesturing

Think/Pair/Share

This strategy offers support for the learner by taking the stress out of class discussions. If the student doesn't know the answer to the question posed, they have the opportunity to learn it from another student. It also helps engage each student in the instruction process.

Students are paired with a think/pair/share (TPS) buddy in class. Once you ask a question, the students think about the right answer and pair with their "buddy" to compare answers. Once prompted, they share the correct answer.

Learning Teams/Cooperative Groups

Like the think/pair/share strategy, dividing students into learning teams provides a support or scaffolding for their learning. Each member should have a designated role or task for which they are accountable. Learning teams work much the same way as TPS buddies; however, student teams discuss a possible correct answer to the question posed.

Hand Signals

This strategy helps keep students engaged. They are required to indicate the correct answer. If they are off task, this strategy helps them refocus.

Students are asked to indicate the correct answer through hand signals. If the question has a yes or no answer, the student can indicate the correct response by holding a thumb up or a thumb down. If there are more choices, students can indicate what they believe to be true by holding up one, two, three, or four fingers.

Take a Stand

This activity allows all students to be involved. It gets them up out of their seats. Ask your students a question that has a yes or no (agree/disagree) answer. They must decide what the correct answer is and stand in a predetermined space that indicates what they believe. For example, you might have one corner of the room for all the *yeses* and the other corner for all the *nos*. You could also use this with more than one answer by providing the answers and they indicate which answer they believe is correct by going to the designated corner or spot.

CHAPTER 2

Spinnerize

You could use the spinner, as seen in figure 2.1, as a whole-class or a group exercise to summarize the end of a lesson. Make a class or group spinner with four quadrants. Label quadrants as "clarify," "explain," "summarize," and "evaluate." You or the students take turns spinning, and wherever the pointer stops, the students must respond. You might use prompts such as those listed below:

Clarify what _____ means.
Explain the concept of _____.
Summarize the _____.
Evaluate how _____ is important in your life.

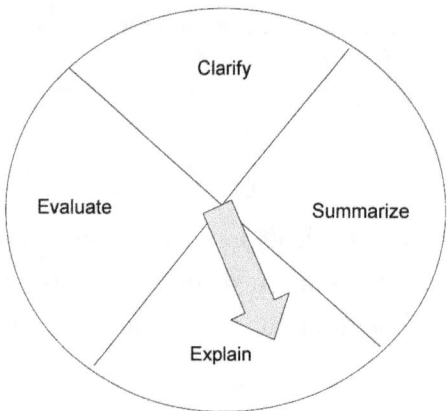

Figure 2.1.

Writing

QAR (Question-and-Answer Response)

This strategy works well to develop critical-thinking skills.

Students work with expository reading material. After reading the material, they are given four questions regarding what they have read. An example can be seen in table 2.2.

Answers are both implicit and explicit in the reading. The first question is a "right there" question. This means that the answer can be found within the text. For the "think and search" question, the student must synthesize the reading to develop the answer. The "author and me" question does not have an answer that can be found in the text. The students must mesh what they already know and what is found in the text. The "on my own" question is also implicit in that students must develop their own answer.

Table 2.2. Question-and-Answer Response

Right there: *I can point to the answer.*	Author and me: *Based on what the author said, I believe. . . .*
Think and search: *I look in several places to find the answer.*	On my own: *This is my opinion.*

20

ASSESSMENT

Interactive Notebook

Students develop their own textbook using a spiral notebook. This tool promotes organization, engagement, and comprehension by combining words and visuals. Students leave several pages at the beginning of the notebook for the table of contents. They number the pages with odd numbers on the right and even numbers on the left. The right side of the notebook is used for teacher input and notes. This might include vocabulary, notes, or questions. The left side of the notebook is the student side. Here they can illustrate and make comments regarding the information provided by the teacher. A pocket can be placed in the back cover for grading sheets.

RAFT: Role, Audience, Format, Topic

This strategy provides a clever way to integrate students' writing and reading. It increases understanding of informational text.

Decide what concept(s) you want the students to understand. Based on the concept, provide them with (1) the role they are to assume, (2) the audience they are to address, (3) the format in which the writing will appear, and (4) the topic for discussion. For example, you may give the following assignment to a biology class:

Role: frog
Audience: tadpole
Format: letter
Topic: life cycle

Using this format, students could be asked to write a letter to a tadpole as if they were a frog. The purpose of the letter is to explain to the tadpole what he can expect to happen as he grows older.

Five Ws Summary

This exercise helps students identify the main points and summarize what they have found. After reading the material, students are given a chart to complete. This chart has them identify who, what, when, where, and why in reference to the text they read.

3-2-1

The 3-2-1 exercise helps students summarize what they have learned and identify what they still need to know. After a lesson, students write three statements that summarize what they have learned, two statements regarding how they can use this learning, and one question they still have.

Having just read an article about recycling, their 3-2-1 might look like this:

3   Recycling is when used materials are processed in order to reduce waste.
     Glass, paper, metal, and plastic can be recycled.
     Recycling helps reduce air and water pollution.

2   I can help reduce energy usage by turning off lights when I leave a room.
I can fix bins to start recycling at home.

1   Where can I find a recycling center?

One-Minute Papers

This is an excellent closure strategy that allows students to process the information they have learned. At the end of a lesson, allow students one minute to write their thoughts about what they have learned. You will probably want to give them a prompt that helps them identify the main idea.

Continuing with the recycling lesson, you might ask students to complete one of the following statements:

Recycling is necessary because . . .
Recycling helps save the planet by . . .

For one minute, they will write all of their ideas in response to the prompt.

Making

Reflective Scale

The reflective scale provides an opportunity for students to self-evaluate. It promotes reflection and ownership of the learning while bringing together concepts.

After an activity or lesson, students complete a reflective scale, as seen in figure 2.2. They indicate on the scale how they feel about the work they completed during class. They also write a statement regarding why they chose that point on the scale.

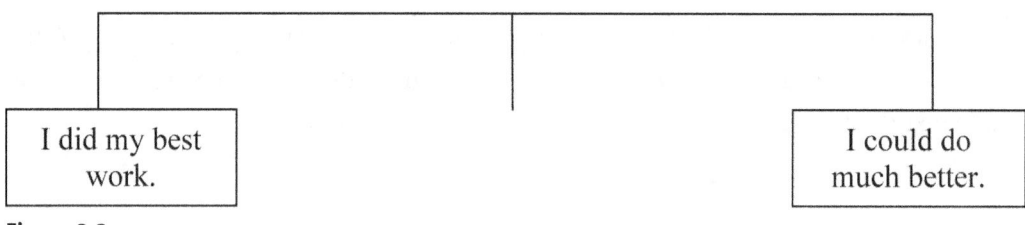

Figure 2.2.

Blog Journaling

Blogs allow students to make, write, and reflect on their own learning. Technology provides a motivational venue to bring learning together. You can view the blog to evaluate how the student is progressing and if they have a clear understanding of the concept or material covered.

There are many free blog sites available, such as www.blogger.com and www.edublogs.org. You will need to set up an account with a username and password. Choose a title. Select a template. Start blogging. You will need to provide response prompts to encourage a quality reflection.

ASSESSMENT

"Jeopardy!"

"Jeopardy!" provides an engaging way to check for understanding or provide a review. Using a PowerPoint program, choose the background desired. The first page is going to be the table. Click on the table icon and highlight enough squares needed for each section. Type in your categories on the first row. Add the point value in the remaining squares. For each point value, click on the number and push *insert hyperlink*. Once you are in the hyperlink window, click on a button on the left that states, "Place in this document." Select where you would like the hyperlink to appear. Next, go to the text box on the top of the window and type in what you want to appear in the hyperlink. Push "OK." Next, start a new slide and type your question. Create a new page and type in your answer. It is important on the answer slide to create a hyperlink back to the first page. After you have typed in your answer, highlight it and create a hyperlink again. Follow the previous instructions. To do this, click on the first page and type the answer you want to appear in the text box. Follow this procedure to finish the rest of the table. Make sure that all the hyperlinks are connected or the game will not work.

Or . . .

Download the program from the site http://teach.fcps.net/trt10PowerPoint.htm. You will need thirty questions in six different categories, plus a "Final Jeopardy" question. Insert the answers and questions into the program. Remember to put the answers before the questions. To use, click on the individual questions in the category. The answer will appear first and students need to provide the question. After the student has provided the question, click on the screen again and the correct question will appear.

Videotape/Audiotape

A videotape or audiotape provides documentation of a student's performance. Students enjoy being taped. They enjoy watching or listening to themselves. They can also view/listen to the tape to self-evaluate based on a rubric and established criteria.

Taping can be used with oral presentations, speeches, role playing, or pantomimes.

Learning Log

A learning log is a student-developed journal that outlines their learning. Students write making connections between content areas or concepts. In some cases, you may want to give a prompt or graphic organizer to help them begin.

These are just a few examples of strategies that can be used for formative assessment. They provide a means for you to do a quick check to determine the level of understanding for your students. Additional ideas can be found at the following websites:

www.lincoln.k12.or.us/Files/Formative%20Assessment%20Strategies.pdf
www.stemresources.com/index.php?option=com_content&view=article&id=52&Itemid=70
www.aliquippa.k12.pa.us/domain/292
http://letthedatabeyourguide.wikispaces.com/Formative+Assessment+Strategies

http://wvde.state.wv.us/teach21/ExamplesofFormativeAssessment.html
http://daretodifferentiate.wikispaces.com/file/view/03+-+Formative+Assessment+Strategies.pdf
http://wths-cff.wikispaces.com/file/view/Formative+Assessment+Tools.pdf

SUMMATIVE ASSESSMENT

When assessment takes place after instruction, it is referred to as summative assessment. If the assessment is valid, it provides a summation of what the student has learned.

Let's take a look at Kirstin and the rest of her second-grade classmates. Before you started your unit on adjectives, you reviewed nouns and verbs. Through a whole-class questioning or recitation (formative assessment), you felt certain that Kirstin and the class understood nouns and verbs. You also used test grades to determine their knowledge base before starting the adjective unit. You modeled the process of describing a person, place, or thing. Using examples on the board, you had students offer descriptive words. You provided sentence strips for each pair of students. They were to identify the noun and the adjective on each strip. Kirstin and her partner correctly identified *beautiful* as the adjective that modified the noun *flower* in the following sentence strip:

The girl picked the beautiful flower.

Given a list of words and a few sentences, the individual students were asked to correctly select an adjective for the sentence. What follows is the exercise Kirstin received:

Directions: Choose a word from the word bank that correctly describes the noun in each sentence.

Word Bank

run	hungry	corner	quickly	fast
pretty	beautifully	delicious	steep	rich
noisily	melting	little	big	older

1. The boy ran to the store.
2. The house sat on the top of a hill.
3. The ice cream cone is chocolate.
4. A dog chewed the bone.
5. Some of the children wanted a pizza.

Upon completion of the exercise, these are the words Kirstin submitted as adjectives.

1. The *quickly* boy ran to the store.
2. The house sat on the top of a *little* hill.
3. The *little* ice cream cone is chocolate.
4. A *hungry* dog chewed the bone.
5. Some of the *noisily* children wanted a pizza.

ASSESSMENT

What can you glean from these answers? Does Kirstin understand the concept of adjectives?

She clearly identifies the noun in each sentence. She is able to pick the noun acting as subject of a sentence but also picks out other nouns. Her answers indicate that she comprehends the words and the sentence meanings. But her answers also indicate that Kirstin is not following through each word. She uses *quickly* instead of *quick* in the first sentence. In sentence 5, she uses *noisily* instead of *noisy*. She is decoding the beginning of each word but not following through to the ending. She does not need additional help with adjectives. At this point, she needs to go back over the words and identify her mistakes. She also needs to slow down in her reading.

In this situation, the teacher felt certain that Kirstin was ready for a summative assessment on adjectives. By dissecting the submitted work, the teacher found that Kirstin needed additional strategies and assistance with follow through and working slower. Additional instructional needs were identified through the summative assessment.

Exercise 2.2

Look at the following examples. What does each student response tell you about their instructional needs? Possible responses may be found at the end of the chapter.

1. Students in a sixth-grade class are working on fractions. They are given the following problem to solve:

   Annie received ½ of the money she earned from selling raffle tickets for the school fundraiser. Charlie received ⅗ of the money he earned from the raffle tickets. Who earned the most money? Explain your answer.

   Leigh's answer: Charlie got more money because 6 is bigger than 5.
   Kemp's answer: I can't tell because they both don't have the same bottom number.
   Pat's answer: I don't know because I don't know how much they each earned.

2. Students in a tenth-grade English class are working on writing an opinion paragraph. They are given the task to state their opinion about a current topic and provide three reasons that support their position. Here are three of the paragraphs that were submitted. What instructional decisions can the teacher make about each of the students?

   Cindy's paragraph: "I believe that snack machines should be available at the school. Snack machines allow students to get a quick bite to eat if they are hungry. The money from the snack machine could be used to give teachers a raise. Kids from the middle school could come over to get something to eat if they were hungry. For those three reasons, I think snack machines should be in the school."

   Donna's paragraph: "I think all people should be free to do what they want. Even if my mom says I can't buy new jeans, I think I should be able to because I need them. I want jeans because my old jeans are not cool."

   Dan's paragraph: "I don't have an opinion on anything. Here are the reasons: I don't know anything. I don't care about anything. I also do not want to learn about anything. That is my opinion."

Whether you use formative or summative assessments, rubrics are helpful in addressing specific criteria. By outlining the specific criteria in the format of a rubric, you provide the students precisely what they need to include in the assignment. Rubrics will be further addressed later in this chapter.

CHAPTER 2

EVALUATION AND GRADING

Evaluating is the process of interpreting the assessment evidence. Based on the evidence provided by the assessment, you make a decision regarding grades.

What is the purpose of grading? Why do teachers grade?

Grading is a form of communication. Grades communicate the student's level of achievement or understanding. The meanings attached to the grades must be clearly stated in order to provide valid and meaningful information. Grades should be based on the established learning targets. By aligning your assessments to the objective or target, you can better validate the student's level of achievement. This criteria-referenced grading indicates to what degree the student has met the criteria or goal.

Grading isn't a clear-cut process. There are always outside factors to consider.

As you work through exercise 2.3, think of the outside factors that may influence the way you grade.

Exercise 2.3

Look at the following gradebook entries. What final grade would you assign for each student? Will each grade count equally? What "red flags" do you see?

Table 2.3. Exercise 2.3 Gradebook Entries

	Homework	Unit project	Test	Test	Test	Quiz	Quiz	Quiz	Behavior	Extra credit	Final
Betty	A	A	90	72	92	82	100	100	B	10	
George	C–	D	81	58	85	60	81	92	D	3	
Anna	B+	B	91	68	85	85	92	98	A	5	
Drew	D	C–	75	78	84	58	90	88	C	0	
Leigh	D	C	85	69	86	67	88	92	C–	7	
Sarah	A	B–	89	65	91	72	100	98	A	0	
Don	A	B	87	70	90	65	88	91	B	5	
Tom	F	D	68	65	71	50	76	80	F	0	

How did you determine the final grade? What problems did you encounter? Would you eliminate any column? Add a column? Can you justify your decisions? What would you do about Tom? What outside factors influenced the grading?

QUALITY ASSESSMENT IS VALID AND RELIABLE

Quality assessment is assessment that meets the needs of the learner and addresses the specific learning targets. Quality assessment is directly linked to the objective or learning target. It is both reliable and valid.

Valid assessment answers the question, "Did I measure what I set out to measure?"

Reliable deals with the consistency of the information that you are assessing. It answers the question, "Are the same results reproducible?"

Practice

Read the following situations. Is the measurement valid? Is the measurement reliable? Why or why not? What problems do you see with each of the assessments?

> Joyce is a student who likes to read and constantly has her nose in a book. She has strong comprehension skills, and although she is an English Language Learner, she is reading on grade level. She is interested in all subjects and enjoys both fiction and nonfiction. You expect Joyce to score high on the comprehension portion of the norm-referenced end-of-the-year state test. For this test, students are asked to listen carefully as a story is read to them. This is followed by five comprehension questions. You are surprised when Joyce scores very low on the test.

In Joyce's situation, she may have trouble understanding the language. She can obviously read the material. The test is not testing her true ability to comprehend since listening may be an outside factor. It is not a valid assessment.

> You have just given a quiz in your fifth-grade science class. You read over the test several times and even take the test to make sure of all the answers. You notice, however, that many students seem confused about the graph indicating the types of rocks. Out of a class of twenty-four students, only two filled in the correct response.

There is obviously a problem with the graph. You need to look at the directions carefully to see if the students understood what was being asked of them. Are you testing graph-reading or are you measuring rock identification? Refer back to the objective. What do you want to measure? Does the assessment tool actually measure the stated objective?

DEVELOPING THE TOOLS

Teacher-Made Tests

A teacher-made test has two types of questions: teacher-constructed responses and student-constructed responses. Teacher-constructed responses use the format where answers are provided by the teacher and the student selects the most appropriate answer. Examples of teacher-constructed responses would include multiple choice, matching, and true/false.

Multiple Choice

Although difficult to construct, the multiple-choice question can assess learning at all levels from knowledge to evaluation. These types of questions are easy to score.

The question or stem should present one problem or question. Each possible answer should be stated in concise terms that are similar in format. Each alternative should be approximately the same length and written in the same style that could make sense if applied to the stem.

For example, look at the following multiple-choice item:

Scuba diving _____.

    A. fun sport that can be dangerous
    B. is best performed in the ocean
    C. requires training and equipment
    D. is always done with a buddy

Do you see some problems? First, the stem is shorter than the alternatives. Alternative A does not form a complete statement. Response B can be confusing since it is a matter of opinion. Scuba diving could take place in a sea, lake, quarry, pool, or any body of water. D should probably be true but the word *always* nullifies the statement. There will be some people who will scuba dive without a buddy. Response C is correct.

How could you rewrite the multiple-choice question to correct the problems?

Check your rewritten question against the following Fisher and Fry (2007, p. 105) checklist for writing multiple-choice questions:

Does each item stem present a meaningful problem?
Is there too much information in the stem?
Are the item stems free of irrelevant material?
Are the item stems stated in positive terms (if possible)?
If used, has negative wording been given special emphasis?
Are the distracters brief and free of unnecessary words?
Are the distracters similar in length and form to the answer?
Is there only one correct or clearly best answer?
Are the items free of clues that point to the answer?

Matching

Matching questions are useful for testing association and recognition. This type of question is written as a group of items divided into two lists: the premise and the response. The student's job is to match corresponding items from the two lists. The lists should center around one general topic. For example, the premise and response could include vocabulary words and their definitions, causes and solutions, events and dates, or books and authors.

Directions should clearly indicate what the student is expected to do. They state where and how the student is to indicate the correct response. They also clarify how many times each response may be used. An unequal number of entries in one of the columns is needed, yet both columns should fit on one page.

ASSESSMENT

Practice

Look at the matching example below. What problems do you see?

Directions: Match the word on the left with the correct synonym on the right.

_____ 1. Help   A. Endure
_____ 2. insipid   B. pounce
_____ 3. persist   C. dull
_____ 4. Repulse   D. Succor
_____ 5. swoop   E. challenge
_____ 6. Contradict   F. reject
_____ 7. Argue   G. debate

The directions do not indicate where the answers should be placed. They also do not designate how many times each definition can be used. The matching does not focus on one subject or topic. There are the same number of words in each column. The format lacks consistency with capitalization. All of the words are verbs, with the exception of one.

How could the matching exercise be rewritten to eliminate the problems?

True/False

True/false questions are written as statements where students must determine if the statement is correct or not. When you write true/false items, include only one concept per statement. Avoid negative statements, especially double negatives. Whether true or false, they should be approximately the same length with approximately the same number of each (positive and negative). Ask students to write out the words *true* and *false* rather than indicate the answer by using a *T* or *F*. Probably the most important rule to remember when writing true/false items is that the statement must be clearly true or clearly false.

Look at the following examples. What problems do you see? How could you rewrite these true/false statements?

1. Major cities are always built near major waterways. (The word *always* makes this statement false.)
2. The New Orleans Saints won the 2010 Super Bowl, which was held in Miami. (This statement is true but could be tricky since it has two parts. Yes, the Saints won, and yes, the game was played in Miami.)
3. Orca whales are members of the dolphin family. (This is a false statement—orcas are whales, but whales are not all dolphins.)
4. It is more important to know where to get information than to know facts. (This statement is opinion. Opinion can be neither true nor false.)
5. Christopher Columbus discovered America. (This is a common belief but not true.)

Student-Constructed Responses

Student-constructed responses use the question format of essay, short answer, or fill in the blank. The answers to the questions are constructed by the student. Let's review some good practices in developing them both.

CHAPTER 2

Essay

Essay questions allow you to form a complete picture of the student's understanding. When writing an essay question, it is better to use several short essay questions rather than one long one. Provide a clearly written question, including the criteria for scoring. Make sure that the question is objective based. In other words, are you actually testing what learning you targeted and is the question worded so you will get the response that you want? How will you score the answer? Are there any restrictions to the answer?

It is a good idea to write out the correct answer and develop a rubric based on your expectations.

Look at the following essay question. What problems do you see? How could you rewrite the question?

The Civil War was a bloody war in the history of the United States. What were some reasons leading up to the war? Were the issues resolved at the end of the war? What was the most interesting battle? Why?

This essay question is all over the place with no clear directions for the answer. This question needs to be broken down into three different questions, such as these listed here:

1. List and explain three of the major reasons for the Civil War.
2. List and explain three results of the Civil War.
3. Explain why the Battle of Gettysburg was a pivotal point in the war.

Written this way, students know exactly what information they need to include. They know how many reasons, results, or explanations must be addressed.

Exercise 2.4

Practice rewriting this essay question.

The caterpillar turns into a butterfly. How?

What would be the model answer? Develop a model answer for your question and establish a rubric based on the criteria that you establish.

Fill in the Blank

A fill-in-the-blank question offers a way to test many facts in a short amount of time. When developing a fill-in-the-blank question, make sure that you provide a clear focus for the desired answer. Avoid wording or grammatical clues. When possible, put the blanks at the end of the sentence and make sure they are approximately the same length.

Look at the following examples. What problems do you see? How could you rewrite these statements?

1. In order for plants to grow, they need _____. (There could be several correct answers here. The statement needs more focus to direct the correct response.)
2. Hurricane Katrina occurred _____. (There could be several correct answers here. The statement needs more focus to direct the correct response.)

3. The Battle of _____ caused the north to _____. (Not enough information is provided.)
4. James Patterson's most exciting book is _____. (This is a matter of opinion.)
5. A popular seasoning for Mexican dishes is _____. (There could be several correct answers here. The statement needs more focus to direct the correct response.)

Each of the previously mentioned assessment tools has a purpose and meets a particular assessment need. The format or type of question changes depending on the type and amount of information needed to indicate student mastery.

Multiple choice can assess many levels of learning. You can test a great deal of knowledge in a relatively short period of time. Multiple choice can be difficult to construct but is easy to grade.

Matching is an excellent way to test factual knowledge or associations. This type of question can measure concepts and different levels of learning. It can be difficult to construct, yet is easy to score.

True/false questions measure a great deal of information in a short amount of time. They are easy to score but sometimes can be unreliable since students are subject to guessing.

Essay questions can measure complex learning. They can assess the thinking process and creativity. They are difficult to create and difficult to score. Without specific directions and rubrics, the correct answers are very subjective. They use a great deal of testing time.

Fill-in-the-blank questions can measure a large amount of knowledge in a short time. It is difficult to measure complex learning with this type of question. They are fairly easy to score but can be somewhat ambiguous.

Exercise 2.5

Read the following statements. Each expresses an assessment need. What assessment tool would be the most appropriate for each?

1. A second-grade teacher wants to find out if her pupils now understand how to form the vowels in cursive writing.
2. A high school social studies teacher wants to know how his students feel about the outcome of the latest election.
3. A fourth-grade teacher wants to know how well his class understands the new science terms.
4. An eighth-grade teacher just finished teaching her students how to compute the volume of a cube. She wants to know how well the students learned the skill.
5. A shop teacher wants to make sure that all his students know the safety precautions when operating a radial arm saw.

PERFORMANCE ASSESSMENT

Performance assessment is an authentic assessment tool. Students demonstrate their understanding through a real-life situation or simulation. It provides an overall or general evaluation of what the student has learned. Isolated skills or knowledge is not measured. This type of assessment allows students to make their learning relevant and applicable to real-world challenges. It involves a process or product that indicates the student's learning. Performance assessments include retellings, presentations, portfolios, and project-based learning.

Retellings include oral-to-oral, oral-to-writing, reading-to-oral, or reading-to-writing retellings. In the first example, the student hears a passage and retells the passage in his own words. Oral-to-writing allows the student to hear the passage and retell the passage in written format. The student may also read the passage himself and retell the meaning orally. In the last example, the student reads the passage and writes the retelling. Retellings offer a means of assessing the student's comprehension of text.

The following list provides useful websites regarding retellings:

www.readinga-z.com/assess/rubrics.html
www.liketoread.com/read_strats_retell.php
http://classroom.jc-schools.net/read/RETELLING.pdf
http://teacher.scholastic.com/lessonrepro/lessonplans/profbooks/strategies.htm
www.louisianavoices.org/unit5/edu_unit5w_story_retelling.html
https://umdrive.memphis.edu/bjcmmngs/public/Models.pdf
www.factsinaction.org/ideas/ideasjul03.htm
www.msu.edu/course/cep/886/Reading%20Comprehension/6Learn_Serv_Proj_StoryRetelling.html

Presentation assessment involves oral reports, role plays, skits, or reader's theater. These venues allow students to practice public speaking and reading.

General guidelines for preparing students to give presentations include the following:

Start with a subject on which they are knowledgeable.
Allow time for practice.
Show students how to refer to notes but not read them.
Model standing with good posture and maintaining eye contact with audience.
Stress no fidgeting or hands in the pockets.

When first beginning oral reports and other presentations, it is a good idea to scaffold the experience by offering initial physical support. You could provide a refrigerator box decorated as a TV or stage. Students can stand inside and give their presentation. You can also provide a plastic microphone. This gives students something to hold onto until their nerves settle or they get comfortable with public speaking.

Role plays, skits, and reader's theater provide opportunities for students to incorporate physical movement with their written dialogue. These strategies not only provide a means for you to assess their understanding but also provide a means to increase their comprehension. These types of presentations are interdisciplinary in nature and can be used in all content areas.

Portfolio assessments house a body of a student's work. This collection can be used to appraise how the student has performed over time. It can be used as a series of best works or as a collection to indicate improvement. Before implementing portfolios, you first decide how you plan on using the material inside. Consider the following questions:

Will it be a summative or formative assessment tool?
What content will be placed in the portfolio?
Will the materials be teacher or student selected?
What format or design will be used?
How will the portfolio be assessed?
Will it include a student reflection?
What specific criteria need to be included on the teacher's rubric?

For additional information about portfolios and their use in the assessment process, see the following websites:

www.pgcps.org/~elc/portfolio.html
www.unm.edu/~devalenz/handouts/portfolio.html
http://jfmueller.faculty.noctrl.edu/toolbox/portfolios.htm
www.teachervision.fen.com/assessment/teaching-methods/20153.html
www.homeedsa.com/articles/portfolios.asp
www.uvm.edu/~jmorris/ep/k12portfolios.html

With any type of performance assessment, it is essential that you use a scoring guide or rubric. Rubrics provide information to the student that clarifies what type of behavior or learning indicators are expected.

If the objective is "TSW give an oral presentation explaining the benefits of recycling," you would want to dissect it to identify what you want the student to know and be able to do. It can be broken into two parts: the presentation and the content. List the criteria you want to see for the presentation. List the criteria you want the student to know for the content. Once you have established the criteria, you can put them in a rubric format. An example of this can be seen in table 2.4.

Table 2.4. Presentation Rubric

4 = Awesome. You did a fantastic job. You met and exceeded all of the criteria.
3 = Well done. You met all of the criteria.
2 = You did well on most of the criteria. There are still a few areas in which improvement is needed.
1 = There is still a great deal that needs improvement.

Criteria	4	3	2	1
Presentation: The student . . . • captures the audience's attention. • speaks clearly and uses expression. • projects voice. • looks at the audience. • has a visual to accompany presentation.				
Content: The student . . . • demonstrates a full understanding of the topic. • provides examples or explanations. • uses appropriate vocabulary relating to the topic. • relates topic to a personal experience. • is able to answer audience questions.				
Comments:				

CHAPTER 2

Rubrics can be difficult to construct but there are many online tools to help. The following list offers a few examples:

www.rubistar.4teachers.org
www.teach-nology.com/web_tools/rubrics
www.rubrics4teachers.com
www,edtech.kennesaw.edu/intech/rubrics.htm
http://school.discoveryeducation.com/schrockguide/assess.html

You first need to decide on the type of rubric. Which type best meets your instruction and assessment needs—holistic or analytic? A holistic rubric, as seen in table 2.5, provides a broad overview of the product. Rather than breaking individual tasks down, this type of rubric looks at the whole process.

Table 2.5. Holistic Rubric

Score	Description
5	Demonstrates complete understanding of the problem. All requirements of task are included in response.
4	Demonstrates considerable understanding of the problem. All requirements of task are included.
3	Demonstrates partial understanding of the problem. Most requirements of task are included.
2	Demonstrates little understanding of the problem. Many requirements of task are missing.
1	Demonstrates no understanding of the problem.
0	No response/task not attempted.

An analytic rubric breaks down the individual components of the assignment. An example is shown in table 2.6. An analysis of the objective is a good place to start when developing an analytic rubric. Identify what criteria the student must meet in each part of the process and the product.

Table 2.6. Analytic Rubric

	Beginning (1 point)	Developing (2 points)	Accomplished (3 points)	Exemplary (4 points)	Score
Criteria #1	developing reflecting beginning level of performance	description reflecting movement toward mastery level performance	description reflecting achievement of master level of performance	description reflecting highest level of performance	
Criteria #2	developing reflecting beginning level of performance	description reflecting movement toward mastery level performance	description reflecting achievement of master level of performance	description reflecting highest level of performance	
Criteria #3	developing reflecting beginning level of performance	description reflecting movement toward mastery level performance	description reflecting achievement of master level of performance	description reflecting highest level of performance	
Criteria #4	developing reflecting beginning level of performance	description reflecting movement toward mastery level performance	description reflecting achievement of master level of performance	description reflecting highest level of performance	

ASSESSMENT

Practice

Read the following learning target and assignment:

Learning target: TSW demonstrate an understanding and appreciation of "going green."

Assignment: Your group's task is to develop a brochure that encourages all people to "go green." You want to include reasons and strategies for "going green." What else would you want to include? What pictures would help illustrate your cause? Where could people find additional information if they need it? The group needs to develop the rough draft on Tuesday. Wednesday, they work on peer reviews and critiques. On Thursday, the group makes edits and corrections. On Friday, they meet in the computer lab to publish the brochure.

How will you evaluate the process and the product? What specific components will you look for in order to assess the learning target?

Other than the content—"going green"—what other objectives could be met through this activity?

Design a rubric that could be used to assess the assignment. How will you hold the group accountable? How will you hold the individual within the group accountable?

ASSESSMENT POINTS TO REMEMBER

- Assessment is a vital component of an aligned curriculum.
- Assessment can be formative or summative.
- Formative assessment guides the instructional process. It allows you to determine if the student is on the right track. This type of assessment lets you know if the student understands the concept or if you need to go back and teach differently.
- Formative assessment is ongoing and takes place in conjunction with instruction.
- Summative assessment occurs at the conclusion of instruction. Once you have confirmed that students understand the material, summative assessment can take place.
- The best practices for assessment development include both teacher-made tests and performance-based tests.
- Teacher-made tests include responses that are teacher made or student made.
- Performance assessment is an authentic assessment that is student centered.
- Rubrics outline criteria and grading for assessment.

EXERCISE ANSWERS

Exercise 2.1

Answers may vary but could include the following:

1. Your capitalization and punctuation is fine. Try to form your letters in a clearer manner to make them easier to read. Go slower and take your time when writing. Let me know if you would like for me to help you practice.

2. Your topic sentence captures the reader's attention and leads into the paragraph very well.
3. The work you showed in the math problem indicated that you understood the concept. Try to work slower to avoid mistakes. Look back through your work and see if you can pinpoint where the mistake was made.
4. You consistently turn in work that is thorough and precise. I can tell that you take time to think through your answers. Keep up the good work.
5. You used some colorful adjectives in your description of the science experiment. Unfortunately, the answer you provided was not correct. Come see me so we can go over the steps.

Exercise 2.2

1. Leigh was on the right track but did not know how to express how the 5 or the 6 related to the problem. She could probably sit down and verbally explain the response. Kemp knows enough about fractions to know that he cannot compare the two fractions as they are written. He needs work on comparing fractions. Pat is the thinker of the group. The teacher would not be able to determine if Pat understood fractions from the response, but the correct response was given.
2. Cindy followed instructions. She wrote a grammatically correct paragraph. The teacher now might want to work on elaboration and descriptive writing. Donna picked a current topic and one on which she has an opinion. She stayed with the same idea throughout her writing but needs help with structure and statements to support her opinion. Don't you just love Dan? He followed the directions and supported his opinion. Dan probably needs to move to more challenging material.

Exercise 2.3

Answers will vary.

Exercise 2.4

Answers will vary.

Exercise 2.5

1. fill in the blank or short answer
2. true/false, multiple choice, essay
3. matching, fill in the blank, or short answer
4. essay
5. true/false, essay, multiple choice

ASSESSMENT

CASE STUDIES

But I'm Not Athletic!

Mr. Will is a first-year physical education teacher at Freeman High School. He walks into his office and realizes he needs to do an assessment before the end of the semester and grades are due in a week. He has already tallied attendance, participation, and dress code. He thinks back to when he was in school and remembers being graded on his performance in physical activity.

He sits at his desk and draws up a simple sheet stating what will be graded and the standards that need to be met. It is not quite the presidential fitness test; however, a grade will be derived based on how many exercise criteria are met.

He lists pull-ups, pushups, sit-ups, the mile run, the shuttle run, and sit and reach. He chooses these exercises because they are the ones used typically for warm-ups. They are also used in the presidential fitness test. He assumes each activity has been practiced over the students' lifetimes.

Mr. Will walks into his first class, which is a freshman class consisting of only males. Some of the students are athletes and some are not. Physical education is a mandated class, which means every student in the school needs a certain amount of PE credits to graduate. Mr. Will runs through the usual warm-ups and gathers everyone around to start the class: "All right, everyone, today and next class, I will be grading you on your strength, aerobic capacity, speed, and flexibility. The test will include pull-ups, pushups, sit-ups, the mile run, the shuttle run, and sit and reach."

The athletes in the class are excited, while the others look a little worried.

Mr. Will adds, "I marked down the scores you need to achieve for certain grades. For example, with pushups you need more than thirty-five for an A, more than twenty-seven for a B, more than twenty for a C, fifteen for a D, and anything less is failing. For the mile, under six minutes is an A, under six minutes thirty seconds is a B, under seven is a C, and under eight is a D. Anything over eight minutes and you fail."

"This will be easy," says Barty, the football team's quarterback, as he wolfs down some chocolate. The others are not so happy; one in particular is Screech Urkel. He moans, "Uh oh, guys, I can't get better than a D on any of these."

Mr. Will separates the class into partners and watches as they count the numbers and mark down their scores. At the conclusion of the second class, Mr. Will looks at all the sheets and records the scores. He notices that the athletes performed well. Some students did well in a few of the exercises. However, many did poorly in all the activities.

He combines these grades with the participation, attendance, and dress code grades. The athletes all had Bs or better. Only a few students had failing grades.

Screech was perfect with the basic grades, having an A in participation, attendance, and dress, but managed only a C after all the grades were averaged together.

Mr. Will was happy that he had his grades in and didn't think twice about his assessment. He felt like he had found an assessment procedure he could use for years to come.

CHAPTER 2

Questions to Consider

1. *What problems do you see with Mr. Will's assessment strategy?*

Mr. Will has not prepared any assessment to measure a predetermined goal. Nor has he given students any prior indication about his assessment techniques. He is measuring physical ability and not knowledge of the subject.

2. *What would be a more appropriate way for Mr. Will to assess his students?*

Mr. Will should have specific objectives and goals that he uses to guide his instruction. Assessment is based on preestablished goals. Students need to know the expectations and criteria they need to meet in order to pass.

3. *What other criteria do you think Mr. Will can implement into his PE classes to help with his final grades?*

He needs to look at state or core standards and determine what the students should know and be able to do. He can then base assessment on that. He also needs to offer a variety of assessment strategies.

ASSESSMENT

Elm Tree

Mrs. Johnston is in her second year of teaching sixth grade at Elm Tree Elementary School. She is an effective teacher to her class of twenty-three students. She strives to meet their individual needs.

Three of the students have been diagnosed with a learning disability. Two of these three have been diagnosed with ADHD. The other student is dyslexic and works with a reading and writing specialist.

The school is located in an urban area, with almost 50 percent of the class living in low-income housing and receiving free or reduced lunch. The class is generally well behaved, yet at times the students get distracted by the few who may have a hard time staying in their seats or are talking too much.

Mrs. Johnston gives very little homework. She found in her first year of teaching that homework assignments were rarely completed. This only caused her frustration. She finds little time in her schedule to cover geography. With an emphasis on reading, writing, and math, it is hard for her to find the time in the day to spend on social sciences. The school is struggling to make AYP, so she feels like she needs to concentrate on the things her administration asks her to focus on. Mrs. Johnston, like most teachers, also has to deal with all the administrative tasks, classroom procedures, and behavior interruptions.

However, she did find time to teach a map geography unit in her class, covering cardinal directions, scale, and symbols. She began the unit by dividing the class into cooperative groups. Each group developed a map of the classroom. They turned these in to her and she reviewed them as a means of formative assessment. All groups seemed to understand the assignment. There were only a couple of groups missing two or three things. She briefly went over these items with the class as she handed back the maps and moved on to the next topic.

She finished teaching the unit and a test was given. The test included identifying the parts of the map and creating a map of their dream bedroom. After she collected and graded the tests, only fifteen out of twenty earned a C- or better and only five of these students received an A. She was surprised that all of the students did not earn a C or better.

Mrs. Johnston shared her concerns with another sixth-grade teacher who used similar lesson plans and a similar test. This teacher's class did considerably better on the assessment. Mrs. Johnston was not sure why her class seemed to do worse than expected on the summative assessment.

After reviewing the test, there did not seem to be one or two poor questions on the test that everyone missed but some sections were not done as well as others. She knew that the unit may have been a little rushed but she felt as if she had no choice, given the language arts and math material she was required to teach.

Questions to Consider

1. *What explanation(s) can you give for the lower-than-expected performance on the end of the unit assessment in Mrs. Johnston's class?*

There a few reasons why the results of the test were lower than expected. The class may not have had as clear an understanding and developed the knowledge as well as Mrs. Johnston had thought. Her only formative assessment was a group activity and her observations. Some individual students may have been depending on the other members of their group rather than having the knowledge themselves. Having only mapped a classroom as a group, mapping a dream bedroom may have been a little difficult for the students.

In addition, the test may not have been adapted to meet the needs of the students with learning disabilities. It also sounds as if the unit was not given the time and attention it needed due to the teacher's time constraints.

2. Was Mrs. Johnston justified in not giving any homework to her students? How might this have helped or hindered their assessment?

Homework can be a matter of opinion. In this case, a homework assignment requiring students to draw a map of their own bedrooms may have benefitted them. This homework assignment could help scaffold them to the "dream bedroom" assessment.

Since class time was limited, this might have been a good situation in which to give homework.

3. How could Mrs. Johnston better use formative assessment to prepare her class for the summative assessment?

Mrs. Johnston could do several things to enhance or add to the formative assessment already in place. First, in using the small groups, she could not only observe but also walk around to the groups and spend a few minutes with each group, giving them feedback and assistance. If a particular group was struggling with a specific aspect, she could ask them individually what each thought they should do and then the group could choose from the individual suggestions. Second, Mrs. Johnston could take notes as she is walking around to the different groups and address any problem areas to the whole class. Third, while the students are working in their groups or doing an anchor activity, she could work one on one with the students who are struggling or have learning disabilities. Finally, if homework were assigned, this could be a valuable formative assessment.

3

INSTRUCTION
Instructional Strategies for Maximum Learning

You have looked at two major instructional components: planning and assessing. Now let's look at how you can deliver quality instruction that aligns with these. There are many factors that can influence the effectiveness of your instruction. Everything from the classroom temperature to what a student ate for breakfast can play a role in how and when learning takes place.

However, for this chapter, we are going to focus on the teacher's role in selecting appropriate and varied instructional strategies.

Your methodology plays a vital role in how well a student learns and retains information. Think about the instructional strategies you currently practice or know. Are the strategies research based? In other words, is there documentation that confirms these strategies help increase learning?

Your choice for instructional method is largely dependent on the objective and the type of knowledge to be learned. For the purpose of this text, we are going to look at instructional approaches or strategies in terms of direct and indirect methods. Direct strategies are teacher centered. They provide explicit instruction. Indirect strategies are more student centered. Students become active in developing meaning.

The strategies you employ need to engage the students in actively learning. Be sure that the strategies are developmentally appropriate, that they are neither too difficult nor too easy for the students' current developmental level. You would not use an abstract-thinking activity with second graders. Developmentally, they are unable to process this type of thinking.

DIRECT STRATEGIES

The goal of direct instruction is to increase student understanding, develop student automaticity in knowledge and facts, and increase the student's ability to transfer knowledge.

Direct approaches are based on the behaviorist theory of learning in that learning can be seen through an observable change in behavior. The teacher is the center of the instructional process.

This type of instruction includes strategies such as lecture presentation, demonstration, questioning, and drill and practice.

CHAPTER 3

Lecture

A lecture format is a type of whole-class instruction. Information is directly given to the students. This type of presentation should be followed by an activity or questioning session in order to increase student comprehension.

Visual aids, including note-taking organizers, aid students' note taking and assist them in identifying important concepts. For example, let's say you are giving notes on the famous battles of the Civil War. One type of note-taking organizer might look like the one shown in table 3.1. By providing this organizer for students, they know which battles are important and what information they need to know. The illustration portion allows them to develop a visual that will help them remember the information.

Quality lectures address specific objectives. They are planned around a series of questions that are discussed within the lecture. Interesting lectures present information in a sequential and engaging manner. They begin by tapping into the student's prior knowledge and move on to develop understanding through the use of stories and analogies. They close with a summary of the main ideas. Here, organizers can help students follow the lecture and identify important components of the topic.

Before giving a lecture, it is a good idea to develop an outline of the lecture topics. This helps establish a framework and guides the lecture into a logical sequence. The outline also helps you keep track of what information is covered.

The following list of sites offers useful graphic organizers:

www.studyzone.org/testprep/ela4/b/takingnotesnonfiction3.cfm
http://edweb.tusd.k12.az.us/templates/summarizing_notetaking.htm

Table 3.1. Battles of Civil War Organizer

Battle	Date	Location	Winner	Significant Event	Illustration
Fort Sumter					
Bull Run					
Monitor and *Merrimac*					
Shiloh					
Harper's Ferry					
Gettysburg					
Atlanta					

INSTRUCTION

www.eduplace.com/kids/hme/k_5/graphorg
www.havefunteaching.com/reading-worksheets/graphic-organizers
www.nvo.com/ecnewletter/graphicorganizers
www.enchantedlearning.com/graphicorganizers
www.readingquest.org/strat
www.teachervision.fen.com/graphic-organizers/printable/6293.html
www.graphic.org
www.teach-nology.com/worksheets/graphic

Demonstration

A demonstration is a type of presentation that allows the speaker to model how something works. To prepare for a demonstration, break the task down into four or five steps. Plan each step ahead of time and practice the procedure or task. Make sure all observers can see you clearly. It is best to try to involve the audience in some way. End the demonstration with a summary.

Using the guidelines previously mentioned, how would you demonstrate each of the following? How could you break each of these activities into four or five steps?

- hitting a golf ball
- making a sandwich
- feeding the cat
- writing a behavioral objective

Questioning

Questioning strategies are another type of direct instruction. This type of instruction can be very effective. Unfortunately, some teachers stick to the comprehension and knowledge questions and never move to the higher level of questioning and learning. Questions such as "What does 'going green' mean?" or "Name one item that can be recycled" are recall questions and do not require higher-order thinking.

Let's look at questioning strategies that you can use in the classroom to expand on the knowledge and comprehension questions.

Questioning can be used to gain more information from a student. You may want the student to provide more detail or expand on their initial answer. Or you may want the student to evaluate the topic or apply the information to another setting. Use prompts such as "Tell me more," "What did you think about that?" "How did that make you feel?" or "Can you describe it?" to deepen the understanding of the content.

Keep the questions simple. Help students focus on the topic if needed. Provide a cue to lead them in the right direction.

Modeling correct responses to open-ended questions will help when you initially begin using different questioning strategies. Let students know the purpose behind the question. Provide opportunities and activities for students to share responses in a small setting rather than the entire class situation.

Think/pair/share is a response strategy that allows students to process the question. You ask the question. Students discuss the answer in pairs. Then they share the answer they have come up with. This facilitates a win-win situation in that all students are engaged and they are offered support through peer interaction.

If you use whole-group instruction and questioning, make sure you provide wait time. Wait time is the three to five seconds after the question is asked before you call on a student. This allows time for students to process and develop a response to what has been asked.

It is a good idea to ask the question and then call on the student. If you say the student's name first, you might lose some of the listeners.

Be careful to practice gender equity when calling on students. Also remember that even the slower students need and want the opportunity to be successful in class. All students deserve the chance to demonstrate mastery and experience success. Encourage students to ask questions about the questions that you ask. Their questions and responses provide excellent formative assessment information. It will help you determine what they know and what needs more instructional attention.

Drill and Practice

In the past, this strategy has earned the reputation of "drill and kill"; however, it is still appropriate in some situations and with some content areas. The drill-and-practice strategy promotes automaticity, which is essential in areas such as multiplication facts and sight words.

The repetitive nature of this strategy reinforces specific skills that can then lead to more complex and meaningful tasks. Mathematics is an excellent example. What others can you think of?

Direct instruction or explicit teaching provides a means to teach specific knowledge or skills efficiently using three major processes: presentation, practice, and feedback. The information to be learned is presented. Students are then provided an opportunity to work with or practice the new information. This is followed by feedback to the students regarding their learning.

INDIRECT STRATEGIES

Indirect instructional approaches are strategies in which students take a major role in the instruction. We are going to look at indirect strategies in three areas: inductive, social, and independent.

Inductive

Inductive approaches focus on reasoning and conclusions. They include strategies such as concept attainment and inquiry-based learning.

Concept attainment engages students in identifying and eliminating both positive and negative statements about a concept. Based on examples provided, the students form a hypothesis or a guess as to what the concept might be. Given additional and more specific examples, they eliminate any guesses that are inappropriate and focus more on the concept. For instance, give the students the following examples of a concept:

liberty	restrictions	curfew	running in a field
incarceration	independence	emancipation	suppression
slavery	choice	no bedtime	

As you go over each word or phrase, place it in the positive or negative category.

Examples of the Concept   *Nonexamples of the Concept*
liberty   restrictions
running in a field   curfew
independence   incarceration
emancipation   suppression
choice   slavery
no bedtime

Based on these examples, the students offer suggestions on what the concept may be.

The concept in this example is *freedom*. Through using this approach, students are able to work with the abstract idea to make it more concrete. They are given multiple opportunities to manipulate and develop the idea.

The list below provides additional sources of information and ideas about concept attainment:

http://olc.spsd.sk.ca/de/pd/instr/strats/cattain/index.html
www.usask.ca/education/coursework/mcvittiej/methods/conatt.html
www.journeytoexcellence.org/practice/instruction/theories/direct/concept.phtml
www.lovinlearning.org/concept

Inquiry lessons are developed around a project or problem. Students are given a question or problem to address. Based on their prior knowledge and guidance from the teacher, they form hypotheses. They gather data to prove or disprove their thoughts. The data is then analyzed to develop a strategy or answer.

Project-based learning and problem-based learning are inquiry approaches that provide authentic situations and relevant learning. While they have much in common, they are two distinct approaches.

In problem-based learning, a specific problem is specified by the teacher. Students work individually or in groups over a designated period of time to develop solutions to the problem. Project-based learning may or may not have a problem involved. Students work collaboratively to develop a project. Project-based learning provides learning opportunities that allow students to make real-world connections.

Both problem- and project-based learning are indirect instructional strategies; however, project-based learning may also fall into the social category. It develops students' skills in collaboration, communication, time management, organization, and use of real-world technology. Project-based learning also provides students with opportunities to integrate subject areas while developing a final product. The last chapter of this text is devoted entirely to project-based learning.

Social Approaches

Social instructional approaches include interpersonal strategies. They involve students working together to meet a goal. They include such strategies as cooperative group, role playing, and panels and debates.

Cooperative group learning is structured, purposeful, and promotes interactive communication. Students are provided with guiding questions or activities that have them working in groups to develop new learning. Prior to working in groups, the students need help in developing their interpersonal skills. They require guidance in learning how to cooperate.

Start with a developmental activity. This activity should help them develop the skills of collaboration. There are numerous ideas available on the Internet. The list below offers some suggested sites:

http://wilderdom.com/games
www.abcand123learning.com/2009/03/life-skills-lessons-cooperation.html
http://findarticles.com/p/articles/mi_qa3934/is_200010/ai_n8905917

Look for activities that promote skills such as taking turns, offering and accepting criticism, listening, compromising, and sharing. Figure 3.1 illustrates one activity that works well.

Group work is more productive when students have a job within the group. Jobs help ensure that each student has a responsibility and will be held accountable. Job titles can vary but you will want to include jobs such as facilitator, recorder, reporter, and materials manager. Each person in the group needs to have a specific and useful job with a written job description that outlines the duties the role entails.

You might use index cards to write the name of the job titles. Write one title per card. Describe the job duties on the reverse side of the card. You can even have students write their names on the job title cards in order to keep track of the jobs each student has had.

Be sure to vary your grouping criteria. Students can be flexibly grouped according to social preference, skill, task, interest, and knowledge base. The grouping strategy will depend on the objective of the activity.

Panels and debates offer an opportunity for in-depth study of an issue. These indirect methods demand that students have a thorough knowledge of the topic. They also encourage the use of higher-order thinking skills as students defend and support their own ideas.

Debates are a form of structured argumentative discussions. They are carried out according to pre-established rules. Debates engage students and assist them in making learning connections. Students are put in a position to analyze, synthesize, and evaluate information. Ideas for debates might include the following:

1. Should your class be permitted to go on a field trip this year?
2. Should students be required to wear uniforms at school?
3. Should you be permitted to choose whatever clothes you want to wear outside of school?
4. Should you be permitted to have a job such as mowing yards or babysitting if your grades are poor?
5. Should you be permitted to purchase or buy whatever you want to with your own money or allowance?
6. Should you be permitted to get any style of haircut you want?

INSTRUCTION

Directions:

Divide the pieces so that one student receives all of the A pieces, one student receives all the B pieces, and so forth.

The object of the activity is to form 4 squares by following these guidelines:

No talking is allowed

One player may give a piece to another player but no player may take a piece without it being offered.

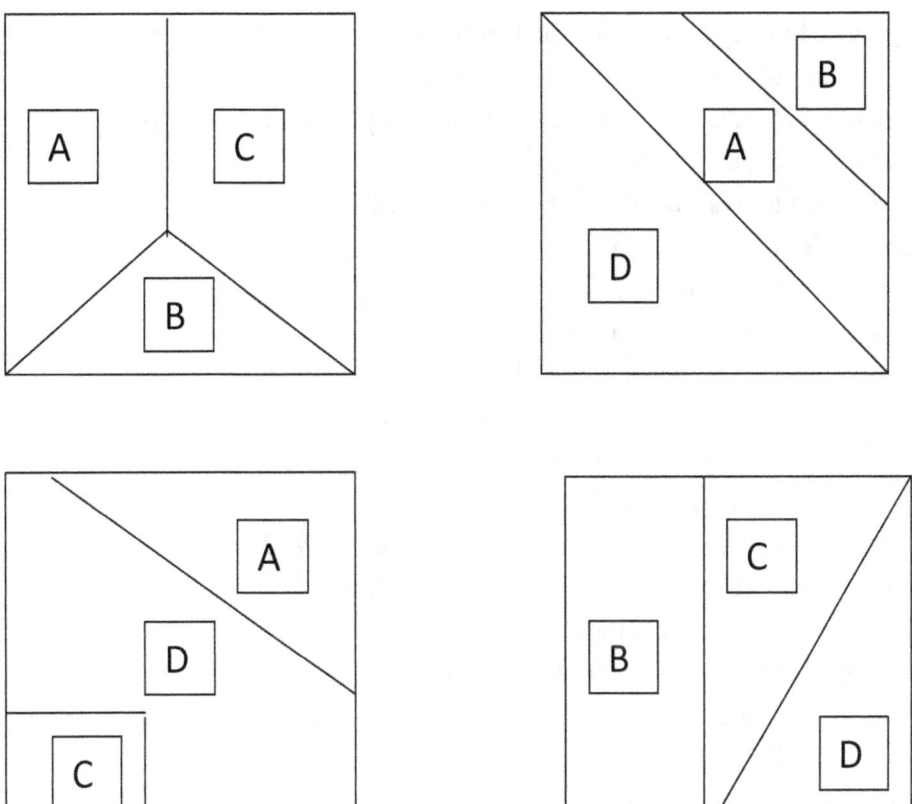

Figure 3.1. Cooperative Group Activity

7. Should you be permitted to have a birthday party and invite friends other than family?
8. Should you be allowed to go anywhere you want to with your friends?
9. Should you be given an allowance or maybe an increase in the amount of your allowance?
10. Should you be permitted to go to a PG-13- or R-rated movie?
11. Should you be permitted to have or attend a sleepover party?
12. Should you be permitted to have a pet?
13. Should you be permitted to join any group you want to—basketball, soccer, Girl Scouts, martial arts, or others?
14. Should you be required to do chores around the house? Which jobs?
15. Should you be permitted to have your own bedroom?
16. Should you have to dress up for those special occasions that your parents feel are important?
17. Should you be allowed to take up any hobby that you want to?
18. Should you be allowed to take lessons to play any musical instrument you'd like?
19. Should you be allowed to stay home when the family goes to visit someone for the day?
20. Should you be permitted to have a TV in your bedroom?
21. Should you be allowed to have your ears pierced or maybe pierce other body parts?
22. Should you be allowed to get a tattoo?
23. Should you be required to wear mandatory bicycle helmets?
24. Should you have homework assignments every night?
25. Should there be corporal punishment at school?
26. Does society have a right to put someone to death?
27. Should you have a curfew? If so, what time and on what days?
28. Should the cafeteria offer fast food lunches instead of cafeteria food?
29. Should school hours be changed to 12:00–6:00 p.m.?
30. Should students be allowed to bring their pets to school?
31. Why is your favorite book better than one the school makes you read?
32. Why should you have the freedom to choose your own bedtime?
33. Why should you be able to watch a certain program?
34. Why should the age to vote, smoke, or drink be raised or lowered?
35. Should kids between the ages of ten and thirteen be dropped off at the mall without adult supervision?
36. Should skateboards be allowed on sidewalks?
37. Should animals be used for scientific experimentation?
38. Should Pokemon cards be allowed in schools?
39. Is television better than books?
40. Should junk food be banned at school?

As you structure the debate, encourage students to use a pros-and-cons graphic organizer. This helps them arrange their thoughts and develop arguments around the specific topic.

Let's say you want students to debate using cell phones in schools. You could use an organizer such as the example in figure 3.2. Using this organizer, students would list the pros and cons. They would be able to identify their position. This would also help them predict the opposing arguments in order to prepare a defense.

INSTRUCTION

My topic is: <u>Cell phones should be allowed in elementary schools.</u>

        Yes because: No because:

Figure 3.2. Debate Organizer

Panel discussions allow for a small group to act as experts in answering the questions posed by students in a larger group. In a classroom setting, students are selected to become "experts" on a topic and are given at least a day to prepare for the discussion. Panel discussions can also be held using outside experts.

When outside experts are invited into the class, make sure students have an understanding of why the visitor is there. It is a good idea to prepare questions for the expert ahead of time. Again, a note-taking organizer will help students follow the discussion and identify pertinent information.

Role playing provides a means for covering a topic in depth and through different perspectives. It helps students explore and increase understanding of feelings and/or actions. You provide background information that explains the situation to be acted out, identify and describe the necessary roles, and set the stage for the action. The activity should be followed by student reflection. Table 3.2 provides an example of a self-reflection rubric. Students explore important components of their own presentation, evaluating their own effectiveness and learning.

Table 3.2. Self-Reflection Rubric

Rating Scale:
5 = strongly agree
4 = somewhat agree
3 = agree
2 = somewhat disagree
1 = disagree

Name:	5	4	3	2	1
I put forth my best effort with this assignment.					
I asked questions when I did not understand something.					
I took responsibility for my own learning.					
I made an effort to keep on top of the assignment and stay ahead.					
I am most proud of:					
I could improve my work by:					

Independent Approaches

Independent approaches are student-centered strategies in which learning is self-directed. Learning centers and independent contracts are two examples.

Learning centers or stations can be an excellent method for engaging students in indirect instruction. They allow students to explore knowledge in a nonintimidating environment. They also provide learning situations located throughout the classroom that focus on small-group or individual activities.

For maximum learning and fewer manageability problems, learning centers need to be highly structured. Provide engaging activities with clearly outlined directions including rotating procedures. Include a means to hold students accountable for their work.

Textbox 3.1 provides an example of a student learning center progress form. Students complete this form to indicate what they have completed within the center.

Centers can be developed to focus on any subject or skill area. They can be used to individualize specific areas of need, reinforce or introduce new concepts, or provide motivation.

> **TEXTBOX 3.1.**
> **Learning Center Checksheet**
>
> ---
>
> Name _____ Date _____
>
> # LEARNING STATION ACTIVITY # _____
>
> **I completed:**
>
>
> **I Learned:**
>
>
> **I can show this learning by:**

Learning contracts are written agreements between the teacher and the student. The students, with teacher assistance, outline the steps they will take to meet the learning objective. Since learning contracts are individual and self-directed, they offer a venue for differentiation. Learning contracts can be used for remediation or enhancement. They provide a means of individualized and independent work. Figure 3.3 provides an example of a learning contract.

INSTRUCTION POINTS TO REMEMBER

- Instruction can be direct or indirect.
- It can be teacher led or student centered.
- The instructional method that you use depends on the objective that you need to meet.
- Direct instructional strategies include methods such as lecture presentation, demonstrations, questioning techniques, and drill and practice.
- Indirect strategies covered in this chapter are discussed in three categories: inductive, social, and independent.
- The inductive process involves a more constructivist approach. Students are guided through the process of using specifics to develop generalizations.
- Inductive approaches include concept attainment and inquiry-based strategies.
- Social instructional methods involve students working together and interacting with the class. Approaches include cooperative discussions, panels and debates, and role playing.
- Learning centers or stations and contracts provide a structure in which students can work independently.

CHAPTER 3

LEARNING CONTRACT

Name _____ Date _____

Topic: _____

Question: _____

To answer my question and learn about this topic, I will:

Read

Write

Develop

Present

Figure 3.3. Learning Contract Examples

LEARNING CONTRACT

Name _____ Date _____

My goal is to:

I plan to do this by:

Resources that I will use include:

I will complete the following activity:

Student signature _____

Teacher signature _____

Figure 3.3. (*continued*)

CHAPTER 3

CASE STUDIES

Not an Average Casey

Casey looks like the average kindergartner. Because she has seven other siblings, she has plenty of exposure to other children. Unlike most of her classmates, she has never been to daycare or preschool. Even though Casey comes from a large family, she is very quiet and introverted. During center time or outside play, she stays by herself and does not interact with other children. She is very hesitant to sit with others on the carpet for circle time and does not like being touched. She will not sit close to other children. When asked questions, Casey refuses to respond, even if the questions are not school related. She only nods.

Casey is a pleasant girl and will follow simple instructions without any problems. At the beginning of the school year, her teacher, Mr. Jacobs, believed that it was just a case of jitters and Casey would outgrow it. However, after two months of school Casey still does not respond to questions or interact with other students.

Mr. Jacobs uses whole-group instruction to teach colors and letters. He reinforces these skills at center time. He also provides time for each student to practice what they have learned. Each student has made a letter book and a number book.

The work that Casey completes in class is inconsistent. A color-by-number can be done without any errors one day and have many the next.

Mr. Jacobs decides to call Casey's mom to gather information that will help him understand Casey. However, he finds that the phone number listed has been disconnected. He decides to ask a colleague for advice and learns that out of the eight children from Casey's family, three have IEPs. His colleague believes social services may be in the process of conducting an investigation of the parents.

Questions to Consider

1. *What problems do you see in Mr. Jacob's approach to Casey?*

Mr. Jacobs should never have let Casey's unresponsiveness continue for two months. He should have contacted the parents long before now. On realizing the phone is disconnected, he should have contacted the school counselor or social worker. There is obviously a problem with Casey.

2. *What problems could Casey be experiencing that would affect her instruction?*

One of the signs of physical abuse is extreme shyness and wariness of others as well as fear of physical contact. Casey may just be shy—it is her first time in school—and while she may be from a large family, she could be afraid to interact with others because she may lack the interaction at home, especially one-on-one time.

Mr. Jacobs needs to look closely for signs of abuse or neglect. He could offer her a snack to determine if she is hungry. He needs to check that she is clean and clothed properly.

INSTRUCTION

3. What instructional strategies might be helpful with Casey?

Mr. Jacobs can only attempt instruction after he has addressed Casey's basic needs and has investigated possible abuse. Once those concerns have been addressed, Mr. Jacobs can attempt to build a rapport with Casey. One-on-one instruction may prove to cross the barriers that Casey has put up. He might even try paired work or work with an older student.

Due to the inconsistent nature of her work, he needs to establish baseline data of her skills. He can only move forward by knowing the starting point of instruction.

CHAPTER 3

Library Bookcase

Ms. Constantine has been teaching fourth graders to use reference books for the last three weeks in the library. She wants to assess her students' understanding of reference books, particularly of atlases, encyclopedias, almanacs, thesauruses, and dictionaries. She needs to determine if the fourth graders have met the state standards. Based on the standards, the students should be able to (a) formulate research questions based on a topic and (b) use appropriate references, such as dictionaries, atlases, almanacs, encyclopedias, and thesauruses, including online, print, and media resources.

Ms. Constantine introduced the students to all of the required reference sources. She even had the music teacher teach them a song about reference sources. She had students use the reference books to find answers to specific questions related to the Civil War unit they were studying.

Students rotated through the different stations; each table was a different station with a different reference book and a specific question. One station was the computer station, where students researched facts in World Book Online. Another station was for encyclopedias, where students developed their own research questions to investigate.

Ernest, a strong reader, found the activities very easy. He found the answers quickly and told those around him the correct responses before they had a chance to look up the information.

Other students, especially Halle and Viola, found the questions difficult to answer. Even working together, they took much longer to complete the assignment and complained that they did not understand the questions.

Ms. Constantine took the questions straight from the workbook and felt sure they were on fourth-grade level. However, she rotated through the tables, helping students to decipher the questions and determine what to look up. She felt mildly confident that 90 percent of the students had mastered her objective.

She reached this determination through informal observations and conversations she had with students at each table. She also assessed by checking their answers. Students were required to come show her their work before they were allowed to check out books at the end of class. She allowed two to three class periods for the work to be completed.

She was pleased with how the lessons came together. She read over the questions the students had generated at the encyclopedia center and felt confident they had an understanding of research tools and how they were used.

Feeling comfortable with their learning, Ms. Constantine used a ready-made interactive quiz to assess students' final understanding of reference books. Some students found this to be fun, but many ended up baffled by the sudden change in format. Ernest fared well on the test since he already felt confident about his knowledge and use of reference books. Both Halle and Viola failed miserably.

Ms. Constantine was disappointed when the final scores were tallied. Only 30 percent of the class indicated mastery of research materials.

INSTRUCTION

Questions to Consider

1. *How could Ms. Constantine have differentiated her instruction to meet the needs of lower-level readers just as effectively as she met Ernest's?*

She could have grouped them heterogeneously so they could provide support for each other. She also needs to assign specific tasks within the group so that students like Ernest would not completely take over.

If she wants to keep homogeneous grouping, she should change the difficulty of the questions. More support is needed in some groups.

2. *How could Ms. Constantine have achieved a higher level of comprehension by tweaking both her instruction and initial formative assessment?*

The entire activity can be more interactive. If she wants to keep her questions the same during the research rotations, Ms. Constantine needs to review the questions beforehand, walking students through the process they are going to go through. For example, she could ask the class what each question means and what they would need to do to find the answer to that question. Clear instruction in preparation for the formative assessment process needs to be provided.

She could engage Ernest as a guide for other students. She could also pair him with Halle or Viola to offer assistance.

Had Ms. Constantine gone through this instructional process more thoroughly and carefully, the students would have gone into the research process with a clearer idea of the activity and her expectations.

3. *What strengths do you see in Ms. Constantine's lesson?*

One of the first strengths in Ms. Constantine's lesson is that she is using the library to meet state standards. She has a hands-on approach to the sources that allows students to interact with the reference materials.

She also connects her material with social studies content from the classroom. In addition, she enlists the music teacher to increase comprehension and retention.

4

ALIGNMENT
A Project-Based Learning Unit

Project-based learning (PBL) is an inquiry-based instructional approach that engages students in cooperative activities. Students collaborate to develop a project in response to a specific goal. You facilitate or coach the process by providing guidance, resources, and some structure.

PBL allows students to integrate content areas while using technology, critical thinking, and problem-solving skills. They work together to develop and present their real-world learning experience. Students become actively engaged in their learning. They learn how to learn.

The twenty-first-century skills movement and Partnership 21 suggest that project-based learning provides a venue to bring together the skills our students need. They classify the twenty-first-century skills into three broad areas: learning and innovation, digital literacy, and career and life (www.p21.org). These skills, taught in the foundation of basic content, help students become collaborators and innovators.

Bernie Trilling and Charles Fadel (2009) offer five key characteristics for effective PBL. They include the following:

- Project outcomes are tied to curriculum and learning goals.
- Driving questions and problems lead students to the central concepts or principles of the topic or subject area.
- Student investigations and research involve inquiry and knowledge building.
- Students are responsible for designing and managing much of their own learning.
- Projects are based on authentic, real-world problems and questions that students care about (p. 109).

The units bring together the elements of an aligned curriculum. The objectives, assessment, and indirect and direct instructional strategies align in order to provide a hands-on authentic student investigation.

If you are looking for guidance, there are a plethora of ideas and resources. It is easy to get overwhelmed with too much information, but here are a few project-based learning resources that might be helpful:

www.pbl-online.org
http://wvde.state.wv.us/teach21/pbl.html
www.edutopia.org
www.envisionprojects.org

www.hightechhigh.org/dc/Projects.php
www.ascd.org/publications/educational_leadership/sept10/vol68/num01/Seven_Essentials_for_Project-Based_Learning.aspx
www.thinkquest.org
www.wested.org/pblnet/exemplary_projects.html
http://pathways.ohiorc.org
http://edtech.boisestate.edu/FIPSE
www.bie.org/pbl/pblhandbook/index.php
http://pblmm.k12.ca.us
www.edutopia.org/php/biglist.php?id=037
www97.intel.com/en/ProjectDesign/UnitPlanIndex/GradeIndex
www.readwritethink.org
www.sciencenetlinks.com/matrix.cfm
http://wise.berkeley.edu/welcome.php
http://coe.ksu.edu/pbl
www.bie.org/videos
www.edutopia.org/project-learning-introduction-video
www.edutopia.org/project-learning-overview-video

The purpose of this final chapter is to outline the developmental process of a PBL unit. Using the PBL unit of "Why Recycle?" you will look at the following:

- Identifying the driving standard(s) and content
- Designing the project scenario and essential question
- Identifying additional content area and objectives
- Determining how students will be assessed
- Planning instructional needs and strategies
- Writing daily lessons

Table 4.1 provides a completed template of the "Why Recycle?" unit. This unit illustrates a six-step process in PBL unit development.

THE SIX STEPS

Step 1: Identify the Driving Standard(s) and Content

It can be difficult to determine which came first—the standard or the content. As with any educational question, the answer is "it depends." In some cases you may start with the content and find standards that fit into the unit. Most likely, you will start with standards and develop a unit that will integrate the content areas.

ALIGNMENT

Table 4.1. Why Recycle? Unit Template

Why Recycle?		
Content area(s): Science, social studies, language arts, math		
Grade level: 3–5	*Duration*: 2 weeks	
Project summary: Students will work in heterogeneous groups to develop a plan that helps the school and classroom environment. Each group will act as a "consultant team" that is hired to develop a plan for helping the school "go green." The presentation must include: • summary of the environmental problem, • explanation of the 3 *R*s (reduce, recycle, and reuse) and how they will help the environment, and • recommendations on how the school can "go green."		
Twenty-first-century themes:	global awareness financial, economic, business, and entrepreneurial literacy civic literacy health literacy environmental literacy	
Unit rationale: This unit provides students with the opportunity to collaboratively explore environmental problems and determine how "going green" can help reduce environmental problems. Students will use guiding questions as a basis for exploring environmental issues and develop a school plan to address these issues.		
Essential questions: What affect do humans have on the environment? Why is it important that we become environmentally aware? How can we each play an active role in helping the environment?		
Content Standards		
Discipline:	*Standards*:	*Assessment*:
	TSW	
science	understand the importance of protecting the environment using the 3 *R*s: reduce, recycle, and reuse.	oral presentation
	collect and analyze data using a variety of means.	worksheet
social studies	demonstrate comprehension of recycling information and construct and explain bar and pie graphs.	oral presentation/PowerPoint
English/language arts	develop and present a persuasive oral presentation using technology.	PowerPoint
	use multiple sources to locate information.	worksheet
	gather information from a variety of print resources.	oral presentation
math	collect, organize, and display data.	worksheet
Assessments		
pre	Introduce the word *environment*. Have students provide examples of an environment. Brainstorm and list ideas on how humans affect the environment.	
formative	observations and discussions peer evaluation self-evaluation	
summative	Each group will present a plan for how the school can implement the 3 *R*s. They will present the plan to the principal. The presentation will involve a PowerPoint that includes the following information: • an explanation of "going green," • the importance of "going green," • one recommendation on how the school can "recycle," • one recommendation on how the school can "reuse," and • one recommendation on how the school can "reduce."	

(continued)

Table 4.1. (*continued*)

	Lesson Plans		
Day 1	• start with pre-assessment • introduction with reading of *The Lorax* by Dr. Seuss • video • distribute group assignments and explain task		
Day 2	Research: Group Rotation		
	Group	*Location*	
	1	library	
	2	classroom research station	
	3	computer lab	
	4	classroom computer station	
Day 3	Research: Group Rotation		
	Group	*Location*	
	4	library	
	1	classroom research station	
	2	computer lab	
	3	classroom computer station	
Day 4	Research: Group Rotation		
	Group	*Location*	
	3	library	
	4	classroom research station	
	1	computer lab	
	2	classroom computer station	
Day 5	Research: Group Rotation		
	Group	*Location*	
	2	library	
	3	classroom research station	
	4	computer lab	
	1	classroom computer station	
Day 6	graphing skills		
Day 7	PowerPoint skills and development in computer lab		
Day 8	practice in groups and peer evaluation		
Day 9	refine and practice		
Day 10	presentations		

For the unit "Why Recycle?" the following environmental studies standard is the driving focus and content.

TSW

understand the importance of protecting the environment using the three *R*s: reduce, recycle, and reuse

Step 2: Design the Project Scenario and Essential Question

With these standards as the focus, the following scenario is developed and given to the students:

> It is election year and the mayor decides to use environmental problems as his platform for the election. He announces to the schools they must develop a plan for "going green" by using the three *R*s.
>
> The principal of your school is somewhat befuddled by this request and turns to the students for help. She asks that they divide into teams and each team develop a plan for going green. She needs to be able to select the best plan to present to the mayor.
>
> The plans include the following:
>
> - clear explanation of "going green" by implementing the three *R*s
> - the importance of "going green" to save the environment
> - three suggestions of recommendations for going green
>
> The plan you design needs to be logical, cost effective, and easy to implement. And there is more. . . . She wants it in a written report and PowerPoint presentation in two weeks!

Step 3: Identify Additional Content Area and Objectives

Next, look at other content areas and standards that integrate with the science core. Table 4.2 outlines the content and standards included in this unit.

Table 4.2. Integrated Content Areas and Objectives

Content Area	Objective(s) *TSW*
science	explain the importance of protecting the environment using the three *R*s: reduce, recycle, and reuse. collect and analyze data using a variety of means.
social studies	demonstrate comprehension of recycling information. construct and explain bar and pie graphs.
English/language arts	develop and present a persuasive oral presentation using technology. use multiple sources to research information on recycling.
math	collect, organize, and display data.

Step 4: Determine How Students Will Be Assessed

As a pre-assessment, introduce the word *environment*. Have students provide examples of an environment. Brainstorm and list ideas on how humans affect the environment.

Formative assessment is ongoing and continuous throughout the duration of the unit. It employs corrective and criterion-based feedback. Observations, discussions, peer evaluation, and self-evaluation are useful tools in formative assessment. It is essential that formative assessment be documented through checklists or anecdotal records. This feedback is used to guide instruction. Examples of an anecdotal record form that can be used to document information and provide corrective feedback can be found in table 4.3.

Table 4.3. Anecdotal Records for Formative Assessment

Criteria	*You could improve this by . . .*	*You have met the criteria because . . .*
Report Contains: • explanations of terms • three logical strategies • no errors • organized content • neat presentation		
Collaboration Demonstrates willingness to: • accept new ideas • work with others • share information and resources • do their part		

Self-reflection and assessment empower students in their own learning. Students can identify their own strengths and areas that need improvement. Table 4.4 provides one example of a self-evaluation tool that could be used with "Why Recycle?"

Table 4.4. Self-Assessment ("Why Recycle?")

Directions: Read the task in the left column. How do you think you did? Rate yourself 1–4.
4 = Fantastic, I did my best.
3 = Good, I put forth effort on this unit.
2 = Okay, but I could do better.
1 = Whew, I really goofed up.

Task	Rating	Fill in this column if you rated 4 or 3. *I am proud of my work because . . .*	Fill in this column if you rated 2 or 1. *I could improve my work by . . .*
Group work			
Written report			
PowerPoint			
Oral presentation			

Summative assessment for the "Why Recycle?" unit includes a presentation and a report component. Since collaboration is such a vital part of PBL units, this area is also assessed. Table 4.5 provides an example of the final unit rubric. Given to the students at the beginning of the unit, the rubric helps guide them toward their goal. It identifies all the components they need to include in their final presentation.

Table 4.5. Final Presentation Rubric ("Why Recycle?")

Scoring:
4 = Awesome. You did a fantastic job. You met and exceeded all of the criteria.
3 = Well done. You met all of the criteria.
2 = You did well on most of the criteria. There are still a few areas in which improvement is needed.
1 = There is still a great deal that needs improvement.

Criteria	4	3	2	1
Oral Presentation				
speaks clearly and uses expression				
projects voice				
looks at the audience				
develops and uses a PowerPoint presentation				
Presentation Content				
explains the term *reduce* as it relates to going green				
explains the term *recycle* as it relates to going green				
explains the term *reuse* as it relates to going green				
explains the phrase *going green*				
clearly explains the importance of going green				
provides one logical strategy the school could use for going green				
uses a bar graph to demonstrate the need for going green				
uses a pie chart to demonstrate the need for going green				
Group Collaboration				
each group member takes part in the presentation				
group collaboration is evident				
all members of the group are prepared to answer questions concerning their topic				

The final grade for the project can be group or individually assigned. A group grade can encourage collaboration. However, accountability measures must be in place so that one student doesn't do all of the work. Group members are assigned jobs and held accountable. Formative assessment plays a vital role in assuring work is being completed and distributed equally. A peer evaluation can also be implemented as a form of documentation. This evaluation, along with your observations and notes, can provide validation if an individual change in grade is warranted.

Step 5: Plan Instructional Needs and Strategies

The "Why Recycle?" unit starts off with a reading of the book *The Lorax*, by Dr. Seuss. This would lead into a discussion about environment and environmental issues. Students would then be given the situation and learning team assignments.

This portion of the unit plots out the instructional timeline. Day 1 is whole group. Days 2–5 are completed as group work. The groups or teams use this time to go to the computer lab, library, research station, or classroom computer. They use this time to gather information and resources. Specific sites, videos, and books are available for reference. All sources relate to the essential question.

Students are guided by a visual plan of group work. An example of this chart is seen in table 4.6.

Table 4.6. Visual Charts for Team Work

Day 2	
Group	Location
1	library
2	classroom research station
3	computer lab
4	classroom computer station
Day 3	
Group	Location
4	library
1	classroom research station
2	computer lab
3	classroom computer station
Day 4	
Group	Location
3	library
4	classroom research station
1	computer lab
2	classroom computer station
Day 5	
Group	Location
2	library
3	classroom research station
4	computer lab
1	classroom computer station

They use a graphic organizer to record information that they will use later in the development of their presentation and report. Table 4.7 provides an example of an organizer.

Step 6: Write Daily Lessons

After the timeline is established, the next step is to develop daily lessons. For days 2–5, students need to understand what they are to do and investigate at each station. Graphing skills are taught as teacher-directed whole-group instruction on day 6.

Table 4.7. Organizer: Do the Research!

Team members:

Question	Answer	Source
What do the following terms mean? 　Reduce 　Reuse 　Recycle		
Why is it important to protect the environment by "going green"?		
What will happen if we don't protect the environment?		

Computer skills and PowerPoint development are taught on day 7. Days 8 and 9 are days to practice, use feedback, and refine.

Day 10 is presentation day. Students have researched, written, developed, and practiced. They are now ready to present their information and ideas for recycling.

ALIGNMENT POINTS TO REMEMBER

This chapter is designed to help bring alignment components together for the development of a project-based learning unit.

- The six steps to develop a project-based learning unit include the following:
  - Identify the driving standard(s) and content
  - Design the project scenario and essential question
  - Identify additional content area and objectives
  - Determine how students will be assessed
  - Plan instructional needs and strategies
  - Write daily lessons

- The driving objective is based in a specific content area.
- Essential questions integrate other subject areas.
- Both direct and indirect teaching methods are needed.
- Students' learning is supported through formative assessment.
- Final grades are clearly outlined through rubrics.
- Both teacher and student know where they are going, how they are going to get there, and how they will know if they have arrived at the destination.

APPENDIX A
Lesson Plan Template

APPENDIX A

Essential Understanding:	
Grade:	Duration:
Description:	
Standard of Learning	*Classroom Objectives*
Summative Assessment:	

Twenty-First-Century Skills

Learning and Innovation

Creativity and Innovation	Critical Thinking and Problem Solving	Communication and Collaboration

Information, Media, and Technology

Information Literacy	Media Literacy	Information and Communication Technology

Life and Career

Flexibility and Adaptability	Initiative and Self-direction	Social and Cross-cultural	Productivity and Accountability	Leadership and Responsibility

Pre-assessment:	
Introduction:	
Instructional Sequence:	Formative Assessment:
Summarize/Close:	
Technology Integration:	
Grouping Needs:	
Differentiation:	

APPENDIX B
Project-Based Learning Unit Template

APPENDIX B

Project-Based Learning Unit		
Content Area(s):		
Grade Level:	Duration:	
Project Summary:		
Twenty-First-Century Themes:		
Unit Rationale:		
Essential Question(s):		
Content Standards		
Discipline:	*Standard:* TSW	*Assessment:*
Assessments		
Pre	
Formative	
Summative	
Lesson Plans		

GLOSSARY

This glossary is meant as a tool to help you decipher some curriculum terms. I have used several sources to attain the definitions in order to provide you with multiple perspectives. As I developed this glossary, I found that my initial premise was validated—education has many names for the same idea and many new names for old ideas.

achievement-based education: *See* outcome-based education. Remember, the labels change as often as needed to keep ahead of critics. (Crossroad)

achievement tests: Tests used to measure how much a student has learned in various school subjects. (Governor)

active learning: A process whereby learners are actively engaged in the learning process, rather than "passively" absorbing lectures. Active learning involves reading, writing, discussion, and engagement in solving problems, analysis, synthesis, and evaluation. Active learning often involves cooperative learning. (Wikipedia)

Any situation in which students learn by moving around and doing things, rather than sitting at their desks reading, filling out worksheets, or listening to a teacher. Active learning is based on the premise that if students are not active, they are neither fully engaged nor learning as much as they could. Some educators restrict the term to mean activities outside of school, such as voluntary community service, but others would say that acting out a Shakespeare play in the classroom is active learning. (ASCD)

affective: A term that refers to emotions and attitudes. (Governor)

affective education: Schooling that helps students deal in a positive way with their emotions and values is sometimes called "affective" to distinguish it from cognitive learning, which is concerned with facts and ideas. Programs designed to help students handle their emotions, which might at one time have been termed "affective education," are now more frequently called social and emotional learning. (NCREL)

alignment: How well the skills and knowledge taught in schools match the requirements of state and/or federal learning standards. (Governor)

The degree to which assessments, curriculum, instruction, textbooks, and other instructional materials, teacher preparation and professional development, and systems of accountability all reflect and reinforce the educational program's objectives and standards. (Schoolwise)

The effort to ensure that what teachers teach is in accord with what the curriculum says will be taught and what is assessed on official tests. If students are not taught the intended content—because of inadequate learning materials, inadequate teacher preparation, or other reasons—or if official tests assess knowledge and skills different from those taught, test scores will obviously be lower than they otherwise would be. For this reason, schools and school districts often devote considerable attention to alignment. In general, this is a desirable practice. However, alignment can be destructive if the process is driven by tests that themselves are inadequate, and if educators feel obligated to teach only what the tests measure. (ASCD)

alternative assessment: Ways other than standardized tests to get information about what students know and where they need help, such as oral reports, projects, performances, experiments, and class participation. (Schoolwise)

aptitude tests: Tests that attempt to predict a person's ability to do something. (Governor)

assessment: Measuring the learning and performance of students or teachers. Different types of assessment instruments include achievement tests, minimum competency tests, developmental screening tests, aptitude tests, observation instruments, performance tasks, and authentic assessments.

The effectiveness of a particular approach to assessment depends on its suitability for the intended purpose. For instance, multiple-choice, true-or-false, and fill-in-the-blank tests can be used to assess basic skills or to find out what students remember. To assess other abilities, performance tasks may be more appropriate.

Performance assessments require students to perform a task, such as serving a volleyball, solving a particular type of mathematics problem, or writing a short business letter to inquire about a product. Sometimes the task may be designed to assess the student's ability to apply knowledge learned in school. For example, a student might be asked to determine what types of plants could be grown in various soil samples by measuring their pH levels. Authentic assessments are performance assessments that are not artificial or contrived. Educators who want assessments to be more authentic worry that most school tests are necessarily contrived. Writing a letter to an imaginary company only to demonstrate to the teacher that you know how is different from writing a letter to a real person or company in order to achieve a real purpose. One way to make an assessment more authentic is to have students choose the particular task they will use to demonstrate what they have learned. For example, a student might choose to demonstrate her understanding of a unit in chemistry by developing a model that illustrates the problems associated with oil spills. (ASCD)

authentic assessment: Alternative tests that assess student ability to solve problems and perform tasks under simulated "real-life" situations. It measures student responses that demonstrate what students think, do, and have become. These outcomes are recorded during normal classroom involvement. Teachers may use handheld computer scanners that scan the students' bar-coded name and responses, then transfer the information into a computer later. (Crossroad)

authentic learning: Schooling related to real-life situations—the kinds of problems faced by adult citizens, consumers, or professionals. Advocates complain that what is taught in school has little relationship to anything people do in the world outside of school; efforts to make learning more authentic are intended to overcome that problem. Authentic learning situations require teamwork, problem-solving skills, and the ability to organize and prioritize the tasks needed to complete the project. Students should know what is expected before beginning their work. Consultation with others, including the instructor, is encouraged. The goal is to produce a high-quality solution to a real problem, not to see how much the student can remember. (ASCD)

authentic task: A school assignment that has a real-world application. Such tasks bear a strong resemblance to tasks performed in nonschool settings (such as the home, an organization, or the workplace) and require students to apply a broad range of knowledge and skills. Often, they fill a genuine need for the students and result in a tangible end product. (NCREL)

benchmarks: A detailed description of a specific level of student achievement expected of students at particular ages, grades, or developmental levels; academic goals set for each grade level. (Schoolwise)

benchmark performances: Performance examples against which other performances may be judged. (NCREL)

blended learning: Learning in a combination of modes. Often used more specifically to refer to courses that use a combination of traditional face-to-face teaching and distance-learning techniques online. (Wikipedia)

brain-based teaching: Approaches to schooling that educators believe are in accord with recent research on the brain and human learning. Advocates say the human brain is constantly searching for meaning and seeking patterns and connections. Authentic learning situations increase the brain's ability to make connections and retain new information. A relaxed, nonthreatening environment that reduces students' fear of failure is considered by some to enhance learning. Research also documents brain plasticity, which is the brain's ability to grow and adapt in response to external stimuli. (ASCD)

character education: An attempt to teach students global or core values. It sounds good, but character qualities such as responsibility, respect, and honesty are redefined to fit the global paradigm. Traditional morality will no longer fit or be tolerated. (Crossroad)

cognitive development: The mental process of acquiring information, building a knowledge base, and learning increasingly advanced reasoning and problem-solving skills from infancy through adulthood. (Crossroad)

cognitive learning: The mental processes involved in learning, such as remembering and understanding facts and ideas. Educators have always been interested in how people learn but are now becoming better informed about cognition from the work of cognitive psychologists, who in recent years have compiled a great deal of new information about thinking and learning. (ASCD)

cognitively guided instruction: An instructional strategy in which a teacher assesses what students already know about a subject and then builds on students' prior knowledge. Students typically are asked to suggest a way to represent a real problem posed by the teacher. Guided questions, encouragement, and suggestions further encourage students to devise solutions and share the outcome with the class. (NCREL)

collaborative learning: An instructional strategy where students of different abilities and interests work together in small groups to solve a problem, complete a project, or achieve a common goal. Also known as *cooperative learning*. (Governor)

community-based learning: Students, faculty, administrators, and community members working together to create new learning opportunities within local communities but generally outside traditional learning institutions. (Schoolwise)

competence tests: Tests created by a school district or state that students must pass before graduating. Sometimes called minimum competency tests, such tests are intended to ensure that graduates have reached minimal proficiency in basic skills. In recent years, some states have replaced minimum competency tests adopted in the 1970s or 1980s with more demanding tests aligned with adopted curriculum standards. (ASCD)

computer-assisted instruction (CAI): Educational programs delivered through the use of computers and educational software. (Governor)

computer-based learning (CBL): Refers to the use of computers as a key component of the educational environment. While this can refer to the use of computers in a classroom, the term more broadly refers to a structured environment in which computers are used for teaching purposes. The concept is generally seen as being distinct from the use of computers in ways where learning is at least a peripheral element of the experience (e.g., computer games and Web browsing). (Wikipedia)

content standards: Standards that describe what students should know and be able to do in core academic subjects at each grade level. (Governor)

cooperative education: A structured method of combining academic education with practical work experience. Research indicates that one of the attributes employers value most in newly hired employees is work experience. A cooperative education experience, commonly known as a "co-op," provides academic credit for career work. Cooperative education is taking on new importance in school-to-work transition, service learning, and experiential learning initiatives. (Wikipedia)

cooperative learning: Small groups of students with varied abilities who learn to share responsibility for achieving group goals. High-achieving students carry the weight of a group assignment for which all receive the same group grade. It is supposed to eliminate competitiveness and individualism while teaching cooperation, problem solving, and responsibility for achieving group success instead of personal success. Promoting collectivism, it lowers academic standards by forcing high achievers to bear the burden of success for others. (Crossroad)

core academic subjects: The academic subjects schools and districts require all students to take in order to be eligible for grade promotion and graduation. (Governor)

core curriculum: The body of knowledge that all students are expected to learn. High schools often require a core curriculum that may include, for example, four years of English, three years of science and mathematics, two or three years of history, one or two years of a foreign language, and one year of health studies. Courses that are not required are called electives.

The term *core curriculum* was used in the mid-twentieth century to refer to a block-of-time program (two or more class periods) in which students and their teacher chose the topics they would study, but few of today's schools have such programs now. (ASCD)

core knowledge: Refers specifically to a reform movement founded by E. D. Hirsch, professor of English at the University of Virginia. The movement is based on the idea that there is a body of knowledge that students and citizens need to know, so school districts should offer a sequential, uniform curriculum. Such a curriculum is outlined in the Core Knowledge Resource Series, a collection of books that specify what students at each grade level should know.

Opponents argue that schools should emphasize the process of learning and the skills of gathering information, and place less emphasis on coverage of particular content. Another argument concerns how to determine the content that all students should learn: Who should decide? On what basis? The inclusion of certain topics, literary pieces, or historic events and the exclusion of others raise issues of cultural bias. (ASCD)

criterion-referenced assessment: An assessment that measures what a student understands, knows, or can accomplish in relation to specific performance objectives. It is used to identify a student's specific strengths and weaknesses in relation to skills defined as the goals of the instruction, but it does not compare students to other students. (Compare to norm-referenced assessment.) (NCREL)

cultural competence: A set of attitudes, awareness, knowledge, and skills that enables effective teaching in racially, culturally, and socioeconomically diverse classrooms. (Governor)

GLOSSARY

culturally appropriate strategies: Practices that celebrate diversity and enable students to succeed in school regardless of race, gender, national origin, religion, age, disability, marital status, family background, or economic status. They sacrifice the rights of individuals to supposedly gain the collective good of the whole. (Crossroad)

curriculum: Although this term has many possible meanings, it usually refers to a written plan outlining what students will be taught (a course of study). Curriculum documents often also include detailed directions or suggestions for teaching the content. Curriculum may refer to all the courses offered at a given school, or all the courses offered at a school in a particular area of study. For example, the English curriculum might include English literature, literature, world literature, essay styles, creative writing, business writing, Shakespeare, modern poetry, and the novel. The curriculum of an elementary school usually includes language arts, mathematics, science, social studies, and other subjects. (ASCD)

developmentally appropriate: Curriculum and instruction that is based on the mental and physical development of the student. (Governor)

differentiated instruction: An instructional technique that includes various ways to teach content and assess learning. It is used to meet student needs and differences in readiness, interests, and learning styles. (Governor)

differentiated schooling: The view that no single form of education is best for all students and all situations. Advocates believe school officials should provide alternative programs and let parents choose among them rather than play "winner take all." (ASCD)

differentiated staffing: The practice of having different instructional roles rather than treating all classroom teachers alike. Various people play a part in the teaching process, but their responsibilities and pay may be greater or lesser than regular teachers. Typical roles include teacher aides, paraprofessionals (or assistant teachers), team leaders, and lead teachers. (ASCD)

differentiated supervision: A system of supervising teachers that depends on factors including their experience, proven teaching ability, interests, and preferences. Some members of the teaching staff may be involved in clinical supervision (intensive analysis of their teaching based on observations of their classroom teaching), while others may propose and conduct their own professional-development plans. (ASCD)

differentiated teaching: Providing for a range of student differences in the same classroom by using different learning materials, assigning different tasks, and using other practices, such as cooperative learning. (ASCD)

discovery learning: The student supposedly generates and tests his own ideas, conclusions, concepts, and so on, creating his own understanding of reality and giving new meanings to traditional words. In reality, he or she is prompted toward a preplanned understanding through stories, suggestions, questions, and group dialogue. (NCREL)

distance learning: Taking classes in locations other than the classroom or places where teachers present the lessons including online, DVD, or telecommuting. (Governor)

Using technology such as two-way, interactive television, teacher(s) and student(s) in different locations may communicate with one another as in a regular classroom setting. (NCREL)

A broad term encompassing technology that extends the learning community beyond the classroom walls. Courses are offered via satellite and the Internet, and email links students directly to peers, professors, programmers, and change agents around the globe. Dustin Heuston of Utah's World Institute for Computer-Assisted Teaching shares his delight in the power of this technology: "We've been absolutely staggered by realizing that the computer has the capability to act as if it were ten of the top psychologists working with one student. You've seen the tip of the iceberg. Won't it be wonderful when the child in the smallest county in the most distant area or in the most confused urban setting can have the equivalent of the finest school in the world on that terminal and no one can get between that child and that computer?" (Crossroad)

environmental education: An educational practice that builds students' awareness of the natural world and how to protect it. (Governor)

essential questions: Basic questions such as "What is distinctive about the American experience?" used to provide focus for a course or a unit of study. Such questions need to be derived from vitally important themes and topics whose answers cannot be summarized neatly and concisely. (ASCD)

exhibition of mastery: A type of assessment in which students display their grasp of knowledge and skills using methods such as skits, video presentations, posters, oral presentations, or portfolios. (NCREL)

experiential education: Education that emphasizes learning from experiences rather than from lectures, books, and other secondhand sources and that may take the form of internships, service learning, school-to-work programs, field studies, or similar experiences. (Governor)

global education: Prepares students to be global, interdependent citizens by developing a global consciousness that embraces "universal" values and pantheistic, earth-centered beliefs that supposedly will save the planet and unify its people. Teaching global idealism and training students in political activism, it builds a malleable young army ready to support the United Nations and other organizations calling for a world government. Watch out! (Crossroad)

hidden curriculum: The habits and values taught in schools that are not specified in the official written curriculum. May refer to what critics see as an overemphasis on obedience, dependence, and conformity. (ASCD)

holistic education: Involving the whole person—body, soul, and spirit. It integrates all subjects and infuses all learning with a pantheistic, monistic spirituality. (Crossroad)

immersion education: A program that teaches children to speak, read, and write in a second language by surrounding them with conversation and instruction in that language. Note that English immersion may differ from other immersion programs. (NCREL)

individualized instruction: A practice providing each student with the lessons and assignments according to her/his strengths and needs. Students work at their own pace to learn the material. Also called individualized education, differentiated curriculum, or differentiated instruction. (Governor)

inquiry-based learning: An instructional method where students create questions about a phenomenon, fact, or piece of literature, and work to answer their questions through an exploration of the topic. (Governor)

integrated curriculum: The practice of using a single theme to teach a variety of subjects. (Governor)

interactive learning: Occurs when the source of instruction communicates directly with the learner, shaping responses to the learner's needs. Tutoring—one teacher teaching a single student—is highly interactive. Computers and other modern technological applications have made it theoretically possible to provide effective interactive instruction to any learner on any subject. (ASCD)

interdisciplinary curriculum: A way of organizing the curriculum in which content is drawn from two or more subject areas to focus on a particular topic or theme. Rather than studying literature and social studies separately, for example, a class might study a unit called "The Sea," reading poems and stories about people who spend their lives on or near the ocean, learning about the geography of coastal areas, and investigating why coastal and inland populations have different livelihoods. Effective interdisciplinary studies have the following elements:

- A topic that lends itself to study from several points of view.
- One or more themes (or essential questions) the teacher wants the students to explore.
- Activities intended to further students' understanding by establishing relationships among knowledge from more than one discipline or school subject.
- Interdisciplinary curriculum, which draws content from particular disciplines that are ordinarily taught separately, is different from integrated curriculum, which involves investigation of topics without regard to where, or even whether, they appear in the typical school curriculum at all. (ASCD)

kinesthetic learning: A teaching and learning style in which learning takes place by the student actually carrying out a physical activity, rather than listening to a lecture or merely watching a demonstration. Building dioramas, physical models, or participating in role playing or historical reenactment are some examples. Other examples include the kindergarten practice of having children perform various motions from left to right in preparation for reading education. (Wikipedia)

learning styles: Differences in the way students learn more readily. Scholars have devised numerous ways of classifying style differences, including cognitive style (the way a person tends to think about a learning situation), tendency to use particular senses (seeing, hearing, touching), and other characteristics, such as whether the person prefers to work independently or with others.

Advocates interpret research as showing that teaching underachievers in ways that complement their strengths can significantly increase their scores on standardized tests. For example, strongly auditory students learn and recall information when they hear it, whereas kinesthetic youngsters learn best through activities such as role playing or floor games. (ASCD)

lifelong learning: A continuous, lifelong program to reeducate the masses in preparation for the twenty-first-century workforce and community. All adults must meet the social, psychological, and work-skills standards required for work and citizenship. (Crossroad).

mastery learning: A psychological process based on the premise that all children can learn if given enough time and help. It uses behavior-modification techniques (stimulus, response, assessment, remediation) to change the students' beliefs, attitudes, values, and behavior. The student must "master" each sequential step toward the required "outcome" (and demonstrate this mastery by modifying behavior patterns) before advancing to the next stage. (Crossroad)

matrix sampling: An assessment method in which no student completes the entire assessment but each completes a portion of the assessment. Portions are allotted to different, representative samples of students. Group (rather than individual) scores are obtained for an analysis of school or district performance. (NCREL)

minimum-competency tests: Tests created by a school district or state that students must pass before graduating. In the 1970s, some states devised minimum-competency tests intended to ensure that high school graduates had achieved minimal proficiency in basic skills. In recent years, states have often replaced minimum-competency tests with more demanding tests aligned with adopted curriculum standards. (Governor)

modeling: The practice of demonstrating to the learner how to do a task, so that the learner can copy the model. It often includes thinking aloud or talking about how to work through a task. (Governor)

multicultural education: Teaching tolerance, "respect and appreciation" for the world's diverse cultures, beliefs systems, and lifestyles—especially those that clash with traditional values and biblical truth—with the acknowledged goal of producing public consciousness of the unity of all things. It shows little tolerance for biblical Christianity. (Crossroad)

multidisciplinary curriculum: Refers to curriculum in more than one discipline or subject area. People may use this term and related ones differently, but, in general, a multidisciplinary curriculum is one in which the same topic (e.g., harmony) is studied from the viewpoint of more than one discipline (e.g., music, history, and literature). For example, students may study weather using a variety of disciplines. They might study the current science behind measuring air pressure, learn about the history of weather prediction, and read and write poetry about weather. (ASCD)

multiple intelligences: A theory of intelligence developed in the 1980s by Howard Gardner that broadly defines intelligence beyond mathematical and linguistic, to include musical, spatial, bodily kinesthetic, and intrapersonal. (Governor)

national goals: The first national goals for education were established initially at a meeting of state governors convened in 1989 by President George Bush and, with minor changes, incorporated into legislation passed in 1994 under President Clinton. The eight goals, none of which were (or could reasonably have been) accomplished, were that by the year 2000:

1. All children in the United States will start school ready to learn.
2. The high school graduation rate will increase to at least 90 percent.
3. All students will leave grades 4, 8, and 12 having demonstrated competence in challenging subject matter, including English, mathematics, science, foreign languages, civics and government, economics, the arts, history, and geography. Every school in the United States will ensure that all students learn to use their minds well so they may be prepared for responsible citizenship, further learning, and productive employment in the modern economy.
4. Students will be the first in the world in mathematics and science achievement.
5. Every adult citizen will be literate and will possess the knowledge and skills necessary to compete in a global economy and exercise the rights and responsibilities of citizenship.
6. Every school in the United States will be free of drugs, violence, and the unauthorized presence of firearms and alcohol, and all will offer a disciplined learning environment conducive to learning.
7. The teaching force will have access to programs for the continued improvement of their professional skills and the opportunity to acquire the knowledge and skills needed to instruct and prepare all students for the next century.
8. Every school will promote partnerships that will increase parent involvement and participation in promoting the social, emotional, and academic growth of children.

New Standards: A joint project begun in 1990 of the National Center on Education and the Economy and the Learning Research and Development Center at the University of Pittsburgh. In 1996, New Standards released a comprehensive set of internationally benchmarked performance standards in mathematics, English language arts, science, and applied learning at the elementary, middle, and high school levels. These were the first integrated set of performance standards in these subject areas developed for national use in the United States. In addition to the standards, the project has also developed a performance assessment system—available in published form as the New Standards Reference Examinations—tied to the standards. Several thousand schools in about twenty states were involved in the creation of the standards and assessments. (ASCD)

norm-referenced assessment: An assessment in which an individual or group's performance is compared with a larger group. Usually the larger group is representative of a cross-section of all U.S. students. (Schoolwise)

opportunity-to-learn standards: Ensure that all students have the resources and conditions they need to reach the same high performance standards. In the mid-1990s, when professional organizations were developing content standards that most people expected would eventually be adopted by the federal government, some educators and politicians argued for parallel adoption of opportunity-to-learn standards, also known as school delivery standards. They contended that if governments proposed to specify minimum standards for what students should know and be able to do, they should also specify what schools must provide students, including curriculum, instruction, and classroom equipment. Opponents argued that they did not want to impose specific requirements but preferred to let local schools decide how best to meet the standards. In the end, standards were not adopted nationally but by the states, which already had minimum requirements, some of which might be interpreted as providing an opportunity to learn. (ASCD)

outcome-based education (OBE): Also called standards-driven education, achievement-based education, and performance-based education. The national, multilevel delivery system for mastery learning. Driven by national standards that match international standards, it forces states and local schools to teach according to national guidelines, curriculum frameworks, work-skills competencies, and so on, by tying much-needed federal funding to compliance. Almost every other definition in this glossary list describes a facet of OBE, so scan the entire list. See also this broader definition of OBE and Outcomes-Driven Developmental Model (ODDM). The latter turned out to be a dismal but expensive failure. (Crossroad)

outcomes: What students are supposed to know and be able to do. (Governor)

pedagogy: The art or profession of teaching. (Governor)

performance assessment: A form of assessment that is designed to assess what students know through their ability to perform certain tasks. For example, a performance assessment might require a student to serve a volleyball, solve a particular type of mathematics problem, or write a short business letter to inquire about a product as a way of demonstrating that they have acquired new knowledge and skills. Advocates believe such assessments—sometimes called performance-based assessments—provide a more accurate indication of what students can do than traditional assessments, which might require a student to fill in the blank, indicate whether a statement is true or false, or select a right answer from multiple given choices.

Evaluating students through task performance can be more time-consuming and therefore more expensive. Most large-scale assessments (such as state testing programs) use this form of assessment sparingly, if at all. But many educators believe it is worth the extra cost because it provides a more accurate and realistic picture of student learning. (ASCD)

performance-based assessment: An assessment system that leans heavily on open-ended answers and extensive writing. According to government research, it often falls short in validity, content, disparate impact, objectivity, and scoring reliability. Dr. E. D. Hirsch Jr. calls it "the original term used by specialists in the psychometric literature for what is called variously 'authentic assessment,' 'exhibitions,' and 'portfolio assessment.'" (Crossroad)

performance criteria: A description of the characteristics to be assessed for a given task. Performance criteria may be general, specific, analytical trait, or holistic. They may be expressed as a scoring rubric or scoring guide. (NCREL)

performance tasks: Activities, exercises, or problems that require students to show what they can do. Some performance tasks are intended to assess a skill, such as solving a particular type of mathematics problem. Others are designed to have students demonstrate their understanding by applying knowledge. For example, students might be given a current political map of Africa showing the names and locations of countries and a similar map from 1945 and be asked to explain the differences and similarities. To be more authentic (more like what someone might be expected to do in the adult world), the task might be to prepare a newspaper article explaining the changes.

Performance tasks often have more than one acceptable solution. They may call for a student to create a response to a problem and then explain or defend it. Performance tasks are considered a type of assessment (used instead of, or in addition to, conventional tests), but they may also be used as learning activities. (ASCD)

placement exam: A skills test given to new students to determine what class or courses are best for their abilities and interests. (Governor)

process-based instruction: The process by which you find an answer is more important than the content. This process is led by a teacher/facilitator trained to provide suggestive questions, then let the students work together toward a consensus. The group's "creative" and collective thinking is what counts. A correct answer is secondary. (Crossroad)

Response to Intervention (RtI): A tool that helps educators identify students at risk for poor learning outcomes, provide evidence-based instructional strategies, monitor student progress, and adjust the interventions in response to students' reaction to the intervention. (Governor)

service learning: Combining community service with politically correct instruction that encourages students to see social problems from a collective, new-paradigm perspective—and to see spiritual differences through the filter of a pluralistic, unbiblical worldview. (Crossroad)

spiral curriculum: An approach to curriculum design that provides for periodic revisiting of key topics over a period of years, presenting them in greater depth each time. It contrasts with mastery learning, which assumes that a topic should be taught thoroughly and mastered before students move on to something else. (ASCD)

standardized tests: Assessments that are administered and scored in exactly the same way for all students. Traditional standardized tests are typically mass-produced and machine-scored; they are designed to measure skills and knowledge that are thought to be taught to all students in a fairly standardized way. Performance assessments also can be standardized if they are administered and scored in the same way for all students. (NCREL)

standards: Statements of what students should know and be able to demonstrate. Various standards have been developed by national organizations, state departments of education, districts, and schools. (NCREL)

transfer of learning: The ability to take previously learned knowledge or skills and apply them to new situations. (Governor)

values education: Teaching children about basic human values including honesty, kindness, generosity, courage, freedom, equality, and respect. The goal is to raise children to become morally responsible, self-disciplined citizens. Because some values are controversial (such as attitudes toward homosexuality), parent groups have occasionally insisted that schools should not attempt to teach values at all. Taken literally, that would be impossible, because for children to live and work together, some values must be communicated and enforced. Character-education programs frequently focus on a set of values arrived at by community consensus. These values may be taught through telling stories, holding discussions, and pointing out examples when they occur.

Values clarification, a form of values education used in some schools in the 1960s and 1970s, has been strongly criticized as misguided and irresponsible. Proponents advised that students should discuss complex value issues (such as who should be thrown from an overloaded lifeboat) while teachers were to remain neutral. Even some of the advocates now admit that, without reasonable adult guidance, values clarification can be harmful. On the other hand, experienced parents and teachers know that, although it is important for adults to be clear about where they stand, students also benefit from opportunities to express their honest views as they think things out for themselves. (ASCD)

work-based learning: Supervised learning activities for students that occur in paid or unpaid workplace assignments, and for which course credit is awarded. Also known as work-site learning. (Governor)

world-class standards: Content and performance levels that are expected of students in other industrialized countries. Also refers to the movement in the United States to bring students' academic achievement and knowledge on par with students' accomplishments in the other industrialized countries.

In 1993, New Standards (a joint project of the National Center on Education and the Economy and the Learning Research and Development Center) began to collect and analyze tests and documents from other countries whose students perform well on international tests and whose citizens perform well economically and tend to hold skilled jobs. The project was based on the view that educational systems are successful when they set clear, consistent, demanding public standards that make sense in the culture of the school and the country. (ASCD)

SOURCES

ASCD: www.ascd.org/Publications/Lexicon-of-Learning.aspx
Crossroad: www.crossroad.to/glossary/education.html
Governor: www.governor.wa.gov/oeo/publications/dictionary.pdf
NCREL: www.ncrel.org/sdrs/areas/misc/glossary.htm
Schoolwise: www.schoolwisepress.com/smart/dict/dict.html
Wikipedia: http://en.wikipedia.org/wiki/Glossary_of_education-related_terms

REFERENCES

Fisher, D., & Fry, N. (2007). *Checking for understanding.* Arlington, VA: Association of Supervision and Curriculum Development.

Harrow, A. J. (1972). *A taxonomy of the psychomotor domain.* New York: David McKay.

Henderson, A., & Berla, N. (1994). *A new generation of evidence: The family is critical to student achievement.* National Committee for Citizens in Education.

Kozloff, M., LaNunziata, L., & Cowardin, J. (2001). Direct instruction: Its contributions in high school achievement. *The High School Journal, 84*(2), 36–54.

Krathwold, D. R., Bloom, B. S., & Masia, B. B. (1964). *Taxonomy of educational objectives: Handbook II: Affective domain.* New York: David McKay.

Mager, R. (1962). *Preparing instruction objectives.* Palo Alto, CA: Fearon.

Marzano, R. (2003). *What works in schools.* Arlington, VA: Association of Supervision and Curriculum Development.

Marzano, R., Pickering, D., & Pollock, J. (2001). *Classroom instruction that works.* Arlington, VA: Association of Supervision and Curriculum Development.

Orlich, D. C., Harder, R. J., & Callahan, R. C. (2007). *Teaching strategies: a guide to effective instruction* (8th ed.). Boston: Houghton Mifflin.

Partnership for 21st Century Skills. (2004). *P21.* Retrieved from www.p21.org.

Pollack, J. (2007). *Improving student learning one teacher at a time.* Arlington, VA: Association of Supervision and Curriculum Development.

Ross, J. (2006, November). The reliability, validity, and utility of self-assessment. *Practical assessment, research and evaluation, 11*(10), 1–8.

Tilling, B., & Fadel, C. (2009). *21st century skills: Learning for life in our times.* San Francisco: Jossey-Bass.

Tyler, R. (1949). *Basic principles of curriculum and instruction.* Chicago: University of Chicago.

ABOUT THE AUTHOR

Suzanne Houff has been an educator for over thirty years. After working as a library media specialist and classroom teacher, she moved into higher education. She is currently a professor of education at the University of Mary Washington in Fredericksburg, Virginia. She specializes in the areas of curriculum, instruction, and classroom management.

www.ingramcontent.com/pod-product-compliance
Lightning Source LLC
Chambersburg PA
CBHW080940300426
44115CB00017B/2898